THE SPIRIT ANIMAL MEDIUM

Channeled Messages, Psychic Healing & the Stories that Changed Lives

By: Veronica Belakova

introduction

I was not the child who grew up talking to animals. Born unwanted in Juárez, Mexico, my earliest memories were not of fairy tales or stuffed toys, but of raw, urgent, and real

survival. Where others saw animals as companions or symbols of magic, I saw only wildness. Creatures of fur and claws. No comfort, no softness. I didn't have the luxury to love them. I didn't have the luxury to even notice them.

The truth is, I saw animals as beasts. They belonged outside, to fend for themselves to make it in the wild, like I did. I write about this life in my first book "My life, My Story, God, you owe me."

In my thirties, a tiny beautiful white ragdoll cat crept her way into my life. She curled up beside the cracks in me and rested there. I didn't know it then, but that little creature planted a seed in my heart.

Then came Ivana. A woman of "funky" color, of light, of big laughter and louder love who turned everything soft. She looked at animals with a reverence I didn't understand. "I just want to travel the world and kiss them all," she told me once on a date, eyes sparkling like a child. "They are God's gifts to this earth, that's why I tattoo them. It's my way of honoring them." I laughed. It all felt so silly to me. I had seen too much, hardened too young. But love has a strange way of making you curious.

Ivana and I began to travel the world. From the mountains of Alaska to the beaches of Thailand, the jungles of Nuku Hiva to the deserts of Madagascar, she sought them out: endemic animals that belonged to sacred places untouched by evolution. She didn't just see them. She felt them. Witnessed them. Spoke to them with her presence. And even kissed some of them! And through her, so did I.

Something began to melt.

I didn't expect this quiet unraveling. I started to see animals not as beasts, but as beings. Mysterious, alien even. Each one carrying its own strange grace, each one reflecting something back to me. They say we become like those we walk beside. And so, I did.
Her awe became my doorway.
Her reverence, my invitation.

I began to see that animals weren't just part of nature they were part of us. They had been placed here by God not just for the earth, but for our healing. Our remembering. Then, during deep meditations that I described in my second book, "Holy Shit I'm a Fu***ng Psychic" animals started appearing. One by one, they came. Guiding me. Grounding me.

Then the Holy Spirit began to guide my eyes. Look at that spider, it said. Look at that beetle.

So, I did. It wasn't about the animal itself, not at first. It was about the moment. The presence. Something sacred was being shown to me, and I couldn't ignore it. I began taking photos, not to collect them, but to remember the exact timing. The exact sequence. I didn't know why then, but I obeyed.

Later, I would scroll through those photos and the animals would speak to me their message. They became my guides, quietly helping me interpret what needed to be heard.

I didn't plan it. I didn't study it. It just became part of my spiritual work. I trusted it.

Eventually, they became my allies in every healing session. Showing up before my clients did, revealing their message before a single word was spoken. Their presence grounded me. I felt I had something solid in my hands.

I still use my feathers too. I write about them in my second book, "Holy Shit I'm a Fu***ng Psychic". I felt armed. I had God and my ancestors. And now, I have the spirit animals, so I began to depend on them. They were not decoration or inspiration. They were medicine. They were instruction.

That is how this book was born.

Within these pages are the spirit animal psychic messages I've delivered over time, each paired with a short story from the session that gave it life.

My prayer is that the words in this book awaken something deep in your soul...

You may hear the call of one of these spirit animals, softly, or like thunder.

If it calls your name, it's because your spirit is ready.

The spirit animal always comes when it's time. Read the message.

Let it sit in your heart.

And when you're ready, walk with it.

Because spirit animals don't just appear they choose you.

And they never leave you the same.

dedication

Like all my books, I dedicate this one to the love of my life, Ivana Belakova.

I wish every psychic healer had someone like you in their life.

You have been my rock, my true confidant. The one who stood by me when I felt like I was losing my mind, when the silence of the spirit world felt too loud, when imposter syndrome crept in, and when loneliness tried to convince me, I was alone.

You didn't just walk beside me you saw my soul when I couldn't.

You stayed when the work got heavy, when my energy was low, when the healer in me needed healing.

You held my hand through the hardest parts of my healing journey... but more than that, you held me up. High, where the birds fly and the angels whisper.

You reminded me of who I am, especially when I couldn't hear my calling clearly.

You took me to places on Earth where I could hear God again.

And when I found peace, you kissed me, and that kiss felt like coming home to myself.

And for all of that... I will forever be grateful.

Thank you for being my light, my anchor, and my safe place....and my interpreter...literally!

disclaimer

1. Like all my books, this one is self-written, self-edited, and self-published, which means you may stumble upon a few typos or odd sentence rhythms. I don't write to win grammar awards. I write to tell my story, from my soul. That means sometimes the words come out raw and unfiltered just as Spirit intended.

2. This book is not polished with perfection; it's polished with presence. Every story, message, and moment captured here is real. The feelings are real. The guidance is real. If you're here looking for a literary masterpiece, this might not be the book for you. But if you're here with an open heart, curious about the unseen world of spirit animals and how they show up in the lives of everyday people... you're in the right place.

3. This book is based on true experiences from my psychic healing sessions. The messages delivered came through during real-life readings, and the stories that accompany them are shared with sacred respect. No names are mentioned, but the truth is all there.

4. Spirit animals speak in symbols, presence, and synchronicities. This book is not a scientific manual it's a spiritual offering. Let it guide you, move you, or even just make you feel something. If a certain animal calls your name, that's your invitation to listen. You're ready.

part 1

In this section, the spirit animals made their powerful and unmistakable presence known. Yet their messages arrived like riddles waiting to be unraveled. I often struggled to find the right words, as if I were piecing together a sacred puzzle. Sometimes their messages came through as full, vivid sentences other times as fragmented words, phrases in reverse, or symbols that only made sense in the moment of the reading. But somehow, when spirit spoke through them, the meaning always found its way to the surface. It was clear, precise, and just what the soul needed to hear.

SLUG

-Take time and enjoy life at a slower pace.
-Slow Down to Reconnect with yourself. Move at your own pace, allowing space for reflection, healing, and alignment with your true self. You don't need to push against the flow, just follow it gently and with patience.
*Embrace the power of stillness -embrace moments of quiet contemplation, to find peace within silence. This stillness allows you to listen to your intuition, recharge your energy, and reconnect with the wisdom within.
*Embody patience and persistence.
-Keep moving forward, even when progress seems slow.
-Trust that every step you take brings you closer to your desired outcome.
-Small, consistent actions will create powerful results.
-Embrace your vulnerability.
-True power lies in your authenticity.
-Trust that vulnerability does not make you weak, it makes you real, and it creates space. for deep emotional connection and growth.
*Let go of the need to control.
-Trust in the unfolding of life's process and allow things to develop naturally. Release the pressure you may be putting on yourself to "get things done."
-Honor the cycles of life.
-Allow yourself to honor the natural rhythms in your life. Trust that rest and rejuvenation are just as important as action. Don't feel guilty for taking time to recharge.
-Move through challenges with grace.
-Cleanse and release old energy.

-Trust in your journey. Your journey is unique, and there is no need to compare it to others.

MOM

I had a client that came to me. She is a big celebrity with sweet energy, you know, the kind that giggles even when life gets heavy. I call them Disney Souls. She was playful, light, but I could tell she carried a lot, like many women do, just in a more polished way.

When we sat together, a man came through dignified, soft-spoken, dressed in a top hat. His presence was graceful, almost from a different era. He came for her.

Not because she knew him, but because he knew her. Her heart, her quiet thoughts, the little insecurities that sometimes whisper into the minds of mothers, of women who nurture, who hold everything together, who sometimes feel like they're not enough even when they're everything. He brought her a gift, not a message of fame or future success, but of reassurance. He told her she'd have a daughter one day. Maybe it was her future, maybe it was energy I was picking up on of something she needed at that moment. I still think about whether that little girl is on her way to earth or if she was a cartoon character living in her imagination. Sometimes readings are like that, they hold space for that particular moment in time.

SCARAB BEETLE

-Be careful with your friends -establish boundaries (Healthy)

-Pay attention to your health.

-Doors of opportunities are being unlocked.

-Blessings on your money are on the horizon, stop stressing.

*Honor your spirituality.

-Quit your bad habit (s) (Drinking and Smoking)

-Be patient and think positive.

*Let go of regrets and anger.

-Your gut feelings and your heart should line up with your actions, otherwise you will continue doing things you regret.

+ Remember you are protected:

-> bad people, negative energies, evil eyes, nightmares etc.

-You are protected-financially, family, relationships, future goals

• Open up and explore – have the freedom to ask yourself, "What is it that you want to do and deserve?

-Stop questioning your luck.

-Rebirth, resurrection, transformation and growth

-Revisit old goals

* Wasting your skills is one of the ways you're keeping yourself away from wealth.

-Living a virtuous life is something you can be proud of.

-Living a life that won't constantly be exposed to others can be fulfilling.

NEVER FORGIVE

In this reading, a woman came to connect with her husband, who had been killed by a drunk driver. She carried a heavy weight of grief, but more than that, anger. It quickly turned to hate as she spoke and then became a barrier, she wasn't willing to release.

As I reached out to the other side, I could feel her husband's presence trying to come through, but there was resistance. Something was blocking the connection.

It wasn't that he didn't want to communicate, it was that he couldn't.

I told her what I felt. She already knew the answer. "I'll never forgive the man who took him from me."

At that moment, Holy Spirit lead me to give her spirit animal's message. I could feel her husband hoping she would listen to the message from the spirit animal.

After, I looked at her and gently said, "Your husband is here. But he can't reach you because of what you're holding onto."

Silence.

She wasn't ready to let go. Not yet. I prayed for her when I finished, and she took with her the spirit animal reading and my advice that healing doesn't happen in anger. Connection doesn't happen if there is hate. The soul communicates in a mediumship session only when there is love.

I can only hope that one day, she will heal.

BEETLE

-Keep going, you are on the right path but have no need to rush.

• You must evaluate the situation in its entirety so that you can find a way to compromise.

-Work with a team to achieve a common goal. Use your creativity and good organization skills to add value.

-Be confident in your abilities.

• It is time to pull out your strengths and share them with the world.

-Don't fight the transition in your life.

-Does your current path deny you of opportunities?

-Seek spiritual nourishment.

- Remember that your fate and destiny never go to sleep. The choices you make in this lifetime determine your destiny.

- Take care of words as well as your actions.

- Learn to be proactive instead of reactive. This way you are able to handle things before they blow up.

-Remember you have a beautiful message within you! Unlock it! You will see that you are extraordinary!

–Unleash this potential and use it to uplift your community.

-Be true to yourself!

-You have the power to participate in unresolved family matters. You can help with the resolution.

- You have a good outcome in this difficult situation. Do not compromise your integrity.

-Right place at the right time

-Be aware of unnecessary haste, take it one day at a time. Give yourself breaks to recuperate from the bustle of modern everyday life. (hectic)
-Embrace change. Discover your own way! Expand your horizons!
-Remember work with others to achieve common goals.

WORK AREAS TO FOCUS ON: sports, addiction, recycle

RECYCLE
In this session I was reminded how perfectly the universe aligns messages when we're open to receiving them. Before my reading, I prayed to God for help and something magical happened. A scarab beetle appeared to me on my gratitude walk. I felt its energy immediately. So, I took a picture and went home to put a message together for my next psychic reading. Later that day, a woman came to me, looking for clarity. She was at a crossroads with her career, unsure of her next steps, feeling lost and disconnected from her purpose. As she spoke, I could feel the weight of her questions. Was she on the right path? Was it time for change? Would things finally fall into place?
As I gave her the message, I watched her face change. Every single message from the scarab directly answered the questions she had about work and life. She sat in silence for a moment, then let out a deep breath, as if something inside her had finally clicked. "This is exactly what I needed to hear," she whispered. She didn't want anything else. Not a cleanse or a mediumship session. She was completely satisfied and ready to continue with her Recycling international business.

CENTIPEDE

-Abundance and good luck

-Transformation or change is coming.

-Remember, even the smallest things have an impact on our lives.

- It is time to connect with your ancestors or the spiritual world.

-You need to make changes.

-Take time to reflect on the love in your life and how you can share it with others.

-Strive to be meek and humble.

-Don't be afraid of death and make sure you make the most of every moment. Don't take time on earth for granted.

-Beware don't take more than you give in your relationships.

-Pay attention in the balance of your life.

-Remember you don't always have to be the biggest or the brightest to make a difference.

-Be mindful of your impact on the world. Even with your smallest actions you can have a big effect.

- Be more careful with your actions and words.

-Embrace your inner peace.

-If you have been at odds recently, reach and to your adversary and make peace while you still can.

-You can act as a mediator of peace between two warring parties, this may be loved ones or friends.

-Obeying this divine message of peace will bring you inner peace.

-You are always protected from evil and unclean spirits.

LEGS OF A CENTIPEDE

Some readings stay with me long after they end. This was one of them. Early one morning, as I finished my meditation, I felt something unexpected, a presence, but not just any presence. A centipede made its way into the slight opening between the baseboard and the carpet and disappeared.

Spirit animals always appear for a reason, and the centipede is a messenger of hidden truths, persistence, and deep transformation. I tapped into this spirit animal, and it gave me a message for my next client.

Afterwards, during my gratitude walk I felt Holy Spirit speaking to me in our own code preparing me for my next session. I knew instantly that this was more than just reading. Someone on the other side was trying to come through. Later that day, a woman came to me for guidance, searching for answers she couldn't quite put into words. During her spirit animal reading, I felt it. Her brother.

His energy was strong and urgent. He had been waiting for this moment. There was something he needed to say, something that had been left unresolved for too long.

I looked at my client and gently said, "Your brother is here. And he has a message for your father."

She nodded. "Go on."

I took a deep breath, allowing the connection to flow. "He says he's been trying to reach him.

Through the phone."

My client's face went pale. "Ok, I will pass on the message."

Then, the energy in the room shifted. The real message came through.

"My death was not an accident. My friend did this. He threw me from the balcony."

A sudden excruciating headache hit me. A pain so intense it stopped me in my tracks. And then, I knew. It wasn't mine. It was his. In that moment, I felt exactly what he had felt, as if his pain had become my own. I saw exactly how he had died. He showed me. He allowed me to feel his pain.

A silence fell over us, heavy with unspoken grief and long-buried suspicion. My client's eye widened. "We always felt something wasn't right," she whispered. "We suspected it, but we never acted on it."

Her brother's energy pulsed with a quiet urgency, but there was no anger, just the need for the truth to be known. For peace.

As the session ended, I could only hope that this revelation brought her family some comfort and closure. Some messages are painful, but they are meant to be heard. And sometimes, the truth reveals itself in the most unexpected ways, even through the legs of a centipede.

BLACK WIDOW SPIDER

-You have the ability to consciously tap into higher knowledge. Allow yourself to use this gift to move forward.

-New beginnings, transformation, and healing.

-It is time to make changes in your life. You have been feeling stuck or stagnant.

-Quick decisions and adjustments must be made.

-Opportunities /change to propel your forward in life

=Recovery / ability to bounce back

*Trust your instincts.

-Be patient with your personal growth.

-You are gifted with a protector and spiritual guide.

-Take a good look at whether or not your ego is out of control!

-Beware the ego is a master of deception, and you will be forced to peel back many layers to get the truth, but it is necessary to be able to discover what your heart is telling you.

-You need to take time to focus on your dreams.

-You have the power to regenerate anything you have lost. (family)

-Beware you tend to repeat cycles simply because your energy loves to recreate emotional attachments.

-You have become so caught up with the drudgery of everyday life, that you forget your dream.

-Take time to create a new reality for yourself. It is the only way to break free.

-Remember you have hidden gifts. It is your responsibility to use them for your own wellbeing.

-Stop feeling inadequate or that you don't deserve it.

- Remember it is all a matter of perception. Look at things from another view. You will see how easy it will be to resolve problems in the future.

-Ask yourself: "What else could this mean?"

-Face your dark side. Accept it for what it is. Shed negativity and start over. New.

- Ba vibrant and authentic. Align with your inner self and your spiritual gifts.

SAY CHEESE

There is a well-known dentist in Beverly Hills. The kind that smiles too wide, but whose soul is begging to be seen. I gave him my psychic book the first time we met. No pressure, just a gift. He was intrigued and you could tell he had questions, but didn't yet have the courage to hear the answers.

Next time I saw him, he flirted with the idea. He said things like, "Tell me all the bad in me. I want to hear it." He hinted, teased, dangled the invitation. But Spirit said no. It wasn't time, and I don't speak unless Spirit opens the door. Then one day, he asked for a session. Official. Clear. I agreed. I prepared it with intention, prayed, and wrote down his spirit animal message. I got in the car and drove in the harsh LA traffic. As I parked by his office, he canceled, last minute. Said he was too busy.

No apology. No respect. He knew I was a healer. He just didn't want it. That's fine. Spirit protected me. Holy Spirit told me: Wrap yourself in light. Place the bubble of God over every appointment with him from now on. So I did.

I saw him again a few times. No mention of the session. Not even a nod. As if it never happened. But Spirit never forgets. Time passed and I heard he was being sued by a celebrity, a big one. Public mess. He had to face exactly what he didn't want to hear that day from me. Spirit will always send the lesson even if the healer isn't allowed to deliver it.

I prayed to water for him, and heard her say, "Some people don't want to change. Some people are addicted to the identity they built inside the web."

Water then said, "Veronica, there comes a moment when life stops allowing you to stay tangled in your own web. The patterns you've repeated for lifetimes, they start to feel heavier, more obvious, harder to ignore. Whether you like it or not, you've been put in position to transform." I knew it far too well.

The Black Widow doesn't punish, she teaches. And when her message is dismissed, life delivers it another way.

WOLF SPIDER

-Lay low until the timing is right.

-Strength and protection – you have the ability to survive in difficult situations.

-You have the subtle but powerful way of standing up for yourself even when others attempt to take advantage.

-Even though you feel small at times, know that you are blessed with power.

-Continue to stand up for yourself, even if it means going against the grain of those around you.

-Remember to stay focused on your goals. Don't give up.

-Pursue your objectives now. Now is the right moment, so it is best to take action using all of your creative abilities.

-Be particular with clear vision of your desires.

-What is it you are afraid of facing? What are you procrastinating?

->Take action and create the life you want.

-Know that your loved ones and your home are protected.

-Find balance in your independence.

-You have the ability to create order out of chaos.

-Call on your helpful guide that can lead the way in difficult times.

FINDING OUR WAY HOME

He walked in with charm, fame, and a name that echoed far louder than the quiet space I had prepared. A successful entertainer, adored by his peers, known for his electric energy. Yet when he sat across from me, his presence felt... mild. Not dull just contained, like he was holding something back. I could see his soul was playful and youthful. It made the energy feel light, almost too light to catch hold of.

The session was clean and polite. Almost vanilla. No dark corners, no unraveling tears, no sudden gasps, or revelations. But beneath the surface, Spirit whispered: "There's more here. He is watching."

Was he testing me? Was I the one shrinking beneath the weight of celebrity? I questioned myself quietly while smiling out loud.

I read the first line from the spirit animal, "Lay low until the timing is right. Know your strength, even if others overlook it."

The reading danced on the surface. But inside, Spirit and I were digging tunnels, sensing that he was afraid to ask the real questions. Maybe he wasn't ready for real answers. Maybe he didn't know what he needed to ask. And that was the lesson.

Spirit doesn't always need a stage to perform. Some messages arrive quietly, like the Wolf Spider in the corner of the room, still alert, waiting for the right moment to strike truth.

And as I closed the session, I thanked him in silence for what I learned. I remembered not to shrink, not to let titles or followers or fame blur my connection to truth. We are all one. All wandering souls, trying to find our way back home.

SNAKE

-This marks the end of one phase of your life and heralds in a new and wise awakening within yourself. Know that this is a transitional period in your life with new spiritual awakenings knocking at your door.

-Know that transformation is now in progress. You will be shedding old skin and emotions and transforming them into something bigger and better.

-Change is in the wind and you are at the center of it all as the catalyst, therefore, to smoothen the process, make sure that your intentions are clear. You must have a clear sense of direction that you wish to strike out.

-Know that these changes are safe. No need to fear them.

-Remember to stay connected to yourself.

-There is information that you require. Observe both the tiny vibrations in the Earth and the warmth and smell of the air and sky. When you learn to connect with your surroundings, you will continue to grow. Thus, you can discard the trappings of the past.

-Remember, there is something mysterious about your gaze, your intensity, and your ability to know what others are thinking and feeling. People find you charming, use it towards your confidence and self-assurance, use this to move in and out of conversations.

-Remember be responsible and benevolent when exercising your power. If you want others to respect you, you must respond to all matters genuinely, from the heart, even when setting boundaries.

-Step into faith when the opportunity comes your way. Don't be afraid your guardian angels are with you.

-Remember what you have gone through you have gone through because you are a strong survivor, along with the help of your gentle guardians. Accept the past and move forward.

-Be mindful of mistruths from others. Always seek out the truth through facts.

-Prioritize spirituality,

-Do not give up or throw out that which may still be quite useful.

GIFT OF TRANSFORMATION

I had a client, an influencer in her field, who came to see me one afternoon. She was one of those people who had everything, or at least it seemed that way on the surface. Her life was full of activity, glamour, and constant movement, everything that many people aspire to have and to be. But beneath it all, there was something else. She felt there was more to her journey that needed to be unlocked.

I had heard that word had gotten out in this age of social media that I had the ability to communicate with animals, and so she, like many others, had come to seek wisdom from the unseen world. Before her reading she told me she wanted me to put together a snake message for her.

Spirit's message for her was gentle. Snake whispered to me that this was a time of deep transformation for her, that an old phase of her life was ending, but the new one had yet to fully unfold. I watched as she absorbed the message. She had already seen a lot of success in her career, but the subtle power of the Snake's wisdom seemed to resonate on a deeper level, calling her to shed the past and to step into a wiser version of herself.

As we continued with the reading, her father came through. He had advice for her regarding some financial moves she was considering. He wasn't here to tell her what to do, but to guide her towards making decisions that resonated with her true heart.

Then, Spirit took me to another person in her life, someone who needed to stay in her circle, someone who would be important in the coming months.

We wrapped up the session with a guided meditation and prayer. I hoped that she had received what she needed for that moment in time, and that she would be able to carry the wisdom of Snake with her as she walked forward.

JAGUAR

-Transformation, adaptability and personal growth
-You have the ability to navigate through life's challenges with ease and perseverance.
- Remember to be flexible in order to achieve personal growth and success in life.
-Partner
-Ask yourself, do you know what environment best nurtures you?
-Beware about what you say and how you say it.
->Leader -stand tall and strong
->You have unlimited potential.
->Let the true you shine - there is no need to demean yourself (appearance) You are sacred, and you have a purpose.
->You are recognizing your own vibrancy.
->You are becoming aware of the sacredness in others.
->Find solitude in time in chaos.
-Be patient. Watch for what is good, right, pleasing, and possible.
-Don't fill your brain to overflowing because it becomes distracting.
->Seek plant magic.
->Earth focused efforts
*Time to realign your thoughts toward positivity.
→ You are ready to move forward with unstoppable force.
-Some aspects of your shadow work are beginning to break through the surface.
*Beware of anything that no longer serves you. Remove and release it.

-Be cautious of the motivation of closest friends.

-Remain vigilant. What may have been safe yesterday, may not be safe tomorrow.

-Set boundaries from harm or disrespect.

->Hidden ailment =judgement or pity

-Clean and purify your home

-Allow the universe to assist in awakening a powerful message inside of you.

PRAY FOR: independence, potential and determination

THIS ONE IS FOR ME

One morning, just like any other, I went into my forest meditation to visit my spirit animals. I've shared about this space in my book, "Holy Shit, I'm a Fu***ng Psychic". My forest, my animals. I love how I touch them, hug them, feel their love wrap around me like old friends I've known forever. But that day was different.

As I stood in stillness, I felt a hidden energy behind some thick tropical leaves. I got closer and the Black Jaguar stepped out.

Its presence stopped me in my tracks. Its beauty wasn't just something to look at it was something that filled my whole body. I started crying with gratitude without even realizing I was crying. It moved toward me slowly, with power and grace, and I bowed my head. That's when it perched its head on top of mine, gently, and the rest of its body covered me like a cloak, like a sacred second skin. It was silent, but I could feel it was telling me: You are seen. You are sacred. You are ready.

When I finished my meditation, I wrote the spirit animal reading like I always do. But this time, Holy Spirit spoke clearly: This one is for you. And I felt it deep in my bones this wasn't a message for a client or the world. It was mine.

People always ask me if I can read myself. I usually say no. Not because I can't, in fact, I haven't even tried. But because I go directly to my Source. I don't need cards or visions to ask God what I need to know. I sit, I pray, I listen, I meditate, I talk to water, I thank every living thing I see, including my body. But that day, that reading wasn't like the others. It held a different weight. It didn't just guide me. It remembered me.

I carry all of my readings with me, even the ones I give to others. But the Jaguar anchored something in my soul. I'm still in awe of it. I'm still thanking it. I'm still wearing it like a crown and a shield. To the Jaguar. To my Source. To my identity. Thank you.

MANATEE

-Slow down and take things more slowly and deliberately.

-Devote time to obtaining peace and stillness. Be mindful of your feelings and find peace and tranquility.

-Stay in touch with your gentle ways even in this competitive and violent world.

-Do not allow the world to alter you in negative ways because if you lose the ability to be calm and solve problems you lose everything.

-Remember it takes a great deal of courage to trust and to be vulnerable, but if you get closed up believing you cant trust, you will put yourself in prison- meaning you will be surviving but not really living.

*Have faith, all will be ok, if you make yourself vulnerable, you will be strong enough to handle it.

*Alligators will always give you the "right away" underwater if not, give them a soft bump.

-Bump off the fear that comes from vulnerability.

-Move between the conscious mind, the material world, and the subconscious mind.

-Remember you can leave the world of your conscious mind and everyday affairs to tap into something greater than Earthly manifestations – which is the Devine.

-The world can desensitize you, so it is easy to lose touch with the miraculous. To regain your sensitivity, you must seek out stillness.

-Float in baths, listen to music, a fountain, or the sound of the sea this will help you find your inner calm and then get in touch with the metaphysical realm.

->You have been blessed with a soothing spirit guide who can bring calm and tranquility into your life.
->Summon into your imagination the manatee when:
- you need peacefulness and tranquility
-in chaotic environments or during stress, or when you get angry
-when you want to trust again after being hurt or taken advantage of to expand your psychic abilities

PRAY FOR: Meditation, transformation, psychic awareness, gentleness, calmness, trust

HOLLYWOOD HILLS, THE DREAM

A big-time YouTuber came to me one afternoon, overwhelmed by the constant pressures of her career. The expectations, the obsessive thinking, the anxiety, and a deep-rooted sense of low-key depression had her spiraling. She had dreamed of living in the Hollywood Hills, a vision she once thought so attainable. Yet, as the years passed, her dreams seemed to be slipping through her fingers, and with every new attempt to climb higher, she felt like she was losing more of herself.

Her energy was heavy that day. It was clear her heart had been burdened by more than just the weight of success or failure. It felt like she was walking in circles, searching for something she couldn't name, trying everything but feeling as if nothing ever quite clicked. I sensed she was caught in the current of her own thoughts, tumbling along with the tide of expectation and exhaustion. This wasn't just about her career; it was about her spirit needing rest, a deep, cleansing stillness to recalibrate.

I laid her down on my medicine blanket and swept my feather gently over her body. I burned palo santo and invited her to close her eyes and let go of the busy world outside. I guided her into a meditation, slowing her breath and led her to a white sandy beach and into the ocean. As the waves of serenity washed over her, I could feel the tension in her chest begin to ease. She was finally letting herself surrender. I cleansed her energy, gently releasing the old, stagnant emotions she had been holding onto.

After the session, she opened her eyes. There was a softness there, a sense of clarity and peace she had been searching for but hadn't known how to access. I connected to God, looked deep into her eyes and told her that I loved her. I know that kind of love made her realize that no amount of chasing fame or success would ever bring peace.

BAT

-Allow yourself to be patient the right moment will come.

-Life is flooded with business activity, chaos = voice inside = take a step back

-Remember that you have the power to adapt to any situation. No matter how painful.

*Teach

*Intuition-trust

-Luck-focus on good

*Survival

*eyesight / clairvoyance / Gift of prophecy

#5

*Seek stillness and meditation.

-Remember your thoughts make and change your realty. Disciple them! Narrow your concentration and prioritize your ideas. ->You will not miss opportunities.

? Ask yourself daily, are you doing what is necessary to achieve satisfaction mentally and spiritually?

-What are you filling your mind with?

-You have a calling! Look deep within yourself.

-Fill your mind with medicine.

? Contentment

*Welcome warm environment

*Cut old partners / lovers out of your life if they are holding you back.

PRAY FOR: belly, hearing

BIG BROTHER

I had a client that came to me one afternoon, but that morning, during my gratitude walk, I saw his brother in a vision. He came to me so clearly that I knew the session that day would be different. When my client arrived, I didn't even have to say much. His brother stepped in immediately. His spirit was strong, calm, and full of love. He showed me the tattoo he got on his ankle before he died. When I mentioned it, I saw my client's face change. That was the moment he knew it was real. That his brother was really with us. It was then that I felt he really opened his heart and his mind. That is the secret to mediumship sessions, our heart and our minds have to be open to love. His brother took over. He spoke through me with so much care. He talked about the weight my client had been carrying: the depression, the addictions, the silence that had been too loud for too long. And then he said something that gave me chills, he said he was okay now. That he had finally found peace. And that he was going to help his brother find it too. I guided him into meditation raw, uncensored, and brutal. We went deep. I helped him release the static in his mind, the racing thoughts, the guilt, the loops. I used prayer and breath. I asked him to allow himself to slow down. Afterward, I sat him on my medicine blanket and did a cleanse to clear what had been stuck for so long. I used herbs and flowers from the forest. I dipped my feathers into water and splashed him. I rubbed salt on his skin and blew on my scared panther to scare the negative energy out of his system because there was so much heaviness in his heart, in his head, in his fascia. But by the end, he looked different. Softer. A little more hopeful. His brother had come not just to speak but to heal.

REINDEER

-Be alert and vigilant of your spiritual sensitivity. It will offer you a keen spiritual vision of future plans.

-Be ready for rare opportunity. Beware opportunity wont last long.

-Avoid unfavorable influences. Look close at everyone you allow around you. Unfavorable influences hurt your life, which is why things go wrong and less than you had hoped for.

>Avoid certain people and environments -ie. Beware of who you listen to on the phone.

-You are concerned about your inactivity of work. The time has come to lighten your load by outlining a future strategy. You will soon receive a promotion that will alter your life and income.

-You will never improve if you consistently refuse to accept responsibility and blame yourself for your mistakes and shortcomings.

->It is time for your transformation. Take complete responsibility for your life choices and results.

*Your heart is good, pure, and compassionate.

>Don't let nasty people's negative energy poison your heart and turn you like them, cynical or malicious.

*You have the universe full support. Continue to be good, innocent, and helpful.

-It is time for you to achieve inner tranquility. It is essential for you to develop a sense of inner calm by accepting serenity within.

-It is time to believe in your inner guidance -> follow your intuition and don't worry about things going wrong.

-It is time for a brand-new journey be curious and excited about this. You are protected and guided for the next state of your life. Start getting ready.

*Tune into the metaphysical world.

->Calm your own mind so that you can be more susceptible to advising on a spiritual level.

-Speak peace, nonviolence, compassion -> you are enlightened.

MOTIVATE THE SOUL

I had a client come to me. She is an international motivational speaker. A woman who had fired up thousands of people with her voice, helping them believe in themselves, push past limits, and dream bigger. She had worked with A-list celebrities, and on paper, her life looked golden.

But when she sat in front of me, I could see in her soul. It was desperate and disappointed, to the point where all I could smell around her was fear.

She had been pouring light into others for years, but her own flame was flickering. She was trying to break into the next level of her career, and the doors were not opening fast enough. The higher she climbed, the heavier the silence became. This wasn't a mediumship session; it was a soul reading. And every word Spirit gave me hit her in the chest like a ton of bricks. Her face stayed composed, but her energy shifted. The truth always lands, whether it's spoken or felt.

I laid her on my medicine blanket and led her through a guided meditation, not to teach her something new, but to help her remember the fire that already lived inside her. To remind her that the same power she gives the world is hers to keep. I know she'll keep going. But my hope is that one day, she stops trying to motivate her soul the way she motivates the masses and instead, just listens to it.

FALCON

*Protection from your spirit guides

• Keep doing what you are doing and be persistent. Show up every day regardless whether or not things are going well.

-Self forgiveness – lack of self-healing is due to the presence of negative energy both in and outside of you.

       -Traumatic event in the past

       ->Let go

       -Focus on self-healing and personal growth

* Find a way to give yourself a boost of energy so that you can continue pursuing your goals.

* Perceptiveness - Increase your sensitivity to the people around you. Don't rush too quickly, think about the outcome or repercussions.

-Get energy from nature.

* Time to take that dream road trip or a flight to Paris.

PRAY FOR: persistence, self-forgiveness, vigor, perceptiveness

STARS, STARS

That morning, on my daily gratitude walk, I saw a vision of a young girl. Then not one but two people in different places wearing NASA logos. I am always in tune for signs, and this one was a slap in the face type of sing, at least for me. Later that day, her mother came to me for a session. The moment she sat, I felt a dense, aching, and unyielding fog of grief surrounding her. And still, her daughter's spirit came through. Sometimes, even through deep pain, souls break through the veil to comfort those left behind. I closed my eyes and returned to the earlier vision. I said, "NASA...NASA." Almost like I was summoning her for answers. Then she lifted me out of my body and showed me the cosmos. I saw stars stretching into infinity. I repeated, "Stars, stars." I opened my eyes with desperation. I connected to God's love then looked into her eyes to give her my love. This always helps people connect. But her mother's eyes stayed closed, her head gently shaking no. Every piece of the daughter's message was lovingly offered, and each one was quietly denied. I closed my eyes and reached out my hand to her daughter to place more information in it. I wanted her mom to feel what I felt from her daughter. Then her daughter gently whispered: "Tell her about the bike. And the cat. He still sees me." I did. And in that moment, something subtle but powerful shifted. Her mother inhaled like she had not breathed in days. A flicker returned to her eyes not full belief, not yet, but a spark. Before I closed in prayer, she admitted that her daughter had passed recently from an infection. That they had matching star tattoos. That was the message: "Stars, stars." The one her mom nodded "No" to.

To the mother, and to all those like her, I offer you this prayer:

May you one day believe the signs your loved ones leave you. May you recognize their voices not with your ears, but with your heart. May you take that road trip, that flight, or even just that moment of stillness, and feel them with you.

And when the grief feels heavy again, look up the stars are still there and so are they.

BEE

-It is time to examine your productivity. Beware disorganization and indecisiveness are probably causing you to miss opportunities.

-Take time to prioritize your goals. Only you can decide which are essential and which are now redundant. Make time for yourself and set schedules. With this in place you will find that your world will become more abundant.

*Remember savoring the fruits of your labor is the reason for work in the first place.

*Remember your industry and hard work produce a community life and social organization that creates abundance. However, remain an individual within this society, in other words reclaim your self-identity and move forward.

-You can accomplish the impossible over and over again.

*Know that we see you carry a heavy burden and will help you with new ideas and projects.

*We know you are seeking a community to belong to. -> We will help you. Your higher self is aiding you and will land you smack in the middle of the sweetest spots.

*Don't forget that miracles happen every day, remember this when the impossible appears by thought.

*JOB – Motivational speaker, healer, lightworker

->Your language of love is important!

*Walk in the middle path = enjoy work and enjoy life.

*Balance work, play, devotion, service, and socialization. At first this may feel overwhelming, but you will figure it out and will become less extreme.
->Get back out there! Work in a group if necessary.
->Draw the honey in your own life. Be innovative and create opportunities based on what you love.

PRAY FOR: action, communication, expectations, industry, productivity, intentions, dreams

SOUND OF HER HEART

I had a woman come to me for a reading. She was a public figure, a light to many, always presenting herself as naturally joyful, grounded, and fulfilled. But the second I touched her hand; I felt it the ache. She was lost. Not recently, not slightly. She had been lost since early childhood. Her smile was practiced, her energy polished, but spirit showed me the exhaustion underneath it all.

She had traveled the world trying to find her happiness. And she did in moments, In places, and in projects. But it was never enough. She had followers on every platform, a tribe in every corner of the internet, but her inner tribe, the one that is supposed to nourish your soul was empty.

Spirit made it clear: she did not need more content, more travel, more validation. She needed balance. She needed to remember the reason she even started, her joy, her service, her voice. So, I led her into a deep hypnotic meditation, a soul retrieval. We traveled together, through the landscapes of her spirit, to find the parts of her that had gone missing. The girl who used to sing to herself in the mirror. The teenager who once dreamed of changing lives, not algorithms. The woman she was becoming if only she had let herself slow down and listen.

Not every session ends with answers. Some only leave you with a compass and a question. But I hope she finds her way back to herself not the self she broadcasts, but the one who truly knows what her heart sounds like in silence.

CROCODILE

This time I did not write anything down. This one was different. We had been asked to visit a woman who needed prayer. Her grief had become too heavy for her to carry alone. On the drive there, the signs began to appear like they always do for me, like scattered breadcrumbs leading me to where I am meant to be. It was not just the sky or the words on passing signs; it was in my breath, my skin, the hum of the air around me. That is how I knew Spirit was preparing me. When we arrived, I felt it immediately. Him. He was already waiting. He did not live there anymore, had not for a while, but his mother had kept his old room just the same. He grabbed my hand not with fear or desperation but gently, like a polite host eager to show me around. His presence was clear and steady, like someone who knew the importance of what was about to happen. Before we even sat in the living room, he said to me: "Go to my room" So I did. He walked me through it with such love. Talking about his bed, his shirts, the way the light hit the shelves. I felt his energy in the little things. Then he said something oddly specific: "Grab that crocodile on the counter." There it was. A small trinket, green, gold, and glittery. At that moment, it was as if a screen turned on behind my eyes. I saw his life, the details, the dreams, the why behind his energy still lingering. We sat in the living room and his mother, tired, cracked open from grief began to speak. And so did he. Through me.

He shared stories, memories, dreams of a shop he wanted to open, filled with exotic fruits and vegetables.

He sent love to his daughter, to his dad, and to his family. He asked us to thank the lady, his neighbor, who found him. That detail broke something open in the room. A tenderness, a peace that started to pour in like light through a crack.

I never needed to write down a spirit animal message for this one. He gave me the message himself. The crocodile was not a metaphor, or a symbol pulled from a vision. It was his. It was real. It held his energy. And through that small object, his spirit activated something in all of us that day. The grief did not vanish. But neither did the love. And maybe that's what this work is really about.

OCTOPUS

-Pay attention to the small things that are draining your energy.

-Not all annoyances are enemies — some are signals.

-What you ignore will keep biting until you address it.

-Be mindful of your boundaries. Who is feeding off your spirit?

-Protection doesn't always look strong — sometimes it's invisible but essential.

-Choose your battles wisely.

-What you attract says a lot about your current state. Cleanse your energy.

-Persistence is your power, keep going, even if you're underestimated.

-Your presence affects others more than you realize.

-Small irritations are leading you to something deeper. Look closer.

-Discomfort is a teacher. Ask what it's trying to show you.

-Be intentional.

LET'S TAKE A SELFIE

There was a woman who repeatedly insisted, firmly, almost like it was her mission, that I come see her in her village. I do not normally make house calls, especially not outside my usual sacred spaces, but something in me said go, so I honored that. The drive was long, over an hour, but the air grew still the moment I arrived. She had a garden, well-kept, perfectly blooming, and I chose that place to sit with Spirit and begin. She was older, the kind of woman who seemed to know a little bit of everything, the kind of woman who had always had the upper hand. Her nails were perfect, her hair brushed and styled like she was about to step on stage. It did not feel like she was meeting a healer. It felt like she was preparing for a performance.

From the first breath of the reading, I sensed something. Boredom, maybe even disappointment. She wasn't really there. She was not connected to the moment. I kept going anyway, even when her silence sat loud in the air. My job is not to convince. I'm the messenger. And when I trust Spirit, I do not doubt the delivery. I placed her into meditation and began to pray over her, letting the weight of energy move across her body in stillness. After the session ended, she suddenly became excited eager even and insisted we take pictures. That made her light up more than the healing itself. And maybe that's okay. Maybe she did not come for a message. Maybe she came to feel seen. Maybe the ritual, the performance, the garden, the photos that was her healing. Some people need answers, others just need presence. In that moment, I gave what I was meant to give, and I left the rest to God.

DOG

-Your heart knows the way. Follow the path of unconditional love, for it is the truest guide.

-You are here to serve and heal. Both through loyalty and through presence.

*Trust your inner knowing , you sense energies before they reveal themselves.

-Embrace your spiritual connection to the Earth. Walk gently, leaving your mark of love and care.

*Communion with the divine can come in moments of stillness, with your head resting, eyes closed, trusting in the moment.

*Spiritual guardianship comes in many forms. You are one for those who cross your path.

*Surrender to the flow of life, knowing that your purpose is deeply intertwined with all beings.

-Listen to your soul's whispers, even when others are too loud — your connection is not dependent on approval.

*You are a mirror of loyalty, wisdom, and trust, teaching others the sacredness of devotion.

-There is healing in silence — in the quiet moments, you reconnect with your true self.

*Cleanse your energy in water.

-Let go of expectations and simply be present. The greatest teachings come in the simplicity of being.

ICE COLD

She walked into the room extremely guarded, like someone who had built her own fortress from years of endurance. Dressed in professionalism, in control, and dressed to show it. She hid her grief behind her medical badge all these years. When I hugged her, I could feel the wall, the armor, the weight she had learned to carry like a sword. Her grief did not weep, it stood still, straight-backed, and sealed shut. She asked to speak to her daughter. I said yes, like I always do, and went searching. In prayer, I asked Spirit to guide me, and I found a name, not the full name, but something close. I offered it gently. She nodded, but I felt her pull back. It was not enough. Not exact. Her pain needed precision, and I had not met it. She sat cold, still hardened, as if even the spirit world owed her more than I had to give. Soon her ice-cold stare frozen the room we sat in, and the session ended. I hugged her again, hoping something in me could still reach her. I thought that would be the end of it. But months later, on one of my morning gratitude walks, her daughter came through in a vision. I was not looking for her, she just arrived. "Tell my mom I like the new book she's reading," she said, with a smile that lingered like sunlight through trees. I carried that message back to her mother. Maybe it touched her, maybe not. She did not say. But I pray for her. I pray that in the quiet moments, when no one is watching, she feels her daughter walk beside her. That she sees her in the mirror, in the books she holds close, in the love that still tries to reach her every single day.

Because some messages don't need to be spoken aloud. Some are wrapped in the silence of devotion. They are loyal, like a dog that waits by the door, steady, always hoping you'll let it in.

part 2

In this part of my book, the spirit animal messages took on a whole new meaning. They weren't just add-ons to my sessions, they were lifelines. I clung to them like breadcrumbs, leading me back home. Each animal came with a message, and I delivered them like I was reading a legal document. At that point in my life, I needed them. I depended on the clarity, the symbolism, the sacred mirror they held up to both me and my clients. I read each line word by word during my reading. From the exclamation points to the arrows and symbols.

Yes, I knew the Holy Spirit was my ultimate guide, that God alone whispered the truth directly into my bones, but I just wasn't ready to let go of the safety net the spirit animal messages provided. Not yet. They gave my sessions structure. They gave my sessions rhythm. And honestly, they gave me confidence.

For several years, those readings became my gospel. Every day was the same, I would rise early, go to the forest on my gratitude walks, and ask God for signs. And those signs... they were nothing short of supernatural. My eyes saw different life in the ordinary clouds. I cried at the sight of the Danube River and at the vibrant green color in the Devin Forest. These walks, my feathers, and the spirit animal messages, built the foundation of what a psychic healing session with me would look like. It wasn't just healing, it was ceremony.

ANT

-Patience, Patience, Patience - What you are asking for or working toward is coming but requires patience and sticking to the path you are currently on.

-Work with diligence and conviction. Work with others to forge your dreams and turn them into reality.

-Consider your role, concentrate on your specialties.

-Make sure you are making the most of your natural gifts.

-You must remain aware that all things are connected.

-Think about how your contributions to your career, family, and day-to-day life fit into the larger picture.

-You are easily able to see your future needs so plan for it.

-You have an intuitive knowledge of how to build your dreams.

-To grow spiritually, you must find significance in small things and learn to appreciate every sign that the universe sends your way.

* Planning-important -spiritual development

*Be flexible spiritually and learn to adapt to life's changes, growths, and transformation.

-Maintain balance between work and rest, this will ensure your work/community thrives.

-Remember, it is very important to find balance in your spiritual and everyday life.

-Effectively communicate with yourself and others to foster understanding and connection.

→ Connect to your ancestors they carry many messages for you to live an easier life.

→You can possess knowledge of the future.

PRAY FOR: Strength, determination, hard work, community, luck, industry, cooperation, strength, focus, devotion

JUST AN ACCIDENT

He came to me quietly, a young man no older than his early twenties, shoulders curled in as if protecting a heart too heavy to carry alone. Diagnosed with psychological problems and social anxiety, he had been labeled and boxed in by the world, but Spirit never sees people that way.

He told me about the challenges of working for his father, about the pressure, the expectations, the silence that grew louder with every passing day. As soon as we began, his sister came through.

It was as if she reached down from the heavens and invited me to sit in the car where her life had ended. She showed me the moment she had died, harsh, quiet, and sudden. She was in the back seat, riding with a friend, and her soul left quickly. No pain, no struggle, no foul play, no drugs, or alcohol. Just an accident. One of those moments where time folds in itself, and life changes forever.

She wanted her brother to know the truth: she had not suffered. And more than anything, she had never left him. She was still with him, especially when he was too anxious to speak or too afraid to breathe. Then, another presence entered the space, his father's friend, now in spirit. This man carried wisdom, and his message was for the father. The Holy Spirit guided me to perform a gentle soul cleanse and a deeper energetic release over his chest. His pain was not just physical, it was grief, pressure, and untold fear pressing into his lungs.

Through hypnosis, I brought in divine breath to loosen the weight and offer release. He softened so much so that he fell asleep. The Ant came forward as his Spirit Animal, reminding us both that patience is a virtue born of quiet strength. That small steps, taken with intention, build empires. His message was not to give up. His role within his family, his workplace, and his spiritual life would one day all make sense. His sister's love. His ancestral line. His purpose was all connected. I left that session praying not for quick change, but for deep-rooted strength, cooperation, and divine timing. Because even when it feels like the world sees you as "less," Spirit knows you are part of something greater.

CELLAR BEETLE

-Play time - joy creates miracles

- Remove yourself from the drama

* Embrace change in the face of life's challenges - you will be renewed after a significant change / challenging period.

->Hidden potential

-Stay true to yourself and have faith

-Challenging yourself or changing you or your beliefs for the sake of others will not help you, you need to put yourself and what you believe in first.

-To help you get through changes you may want to find help in your community and those who you identify with that truly support you, there you will find the strength and understanding which will help you get through your problem.

• Stand still and pay close attention, look around, there may be something happening around you that you are not fully aware of.

-Time to find and improve your spirituality

-Remember you are stronger than you appear

-You can accomplish much more when you unite with others - "your people"

• Never give up!

-Remember that not everything is lost as long as you keep fighting!

PRAY FOR: Adaptation, blessings, abundance

FINDING HER WAY BACK TO JOY

Sometimes people come for a reading not expecting much. They are curious, maybe a little numb, just hoping to feel something real. She was like that quiet, a little guarded, almost like she was carrying too much but didn't know where to put it down. As I opened the space, her energy was heavy but patient, like a part of her was still hoping for a miracle. Then, a man stepped forward, a dear friend who had passed. His presence was full of laughter, teasing energy, and shared memories. He showed me scenes of trips they took together, wild, and carefree, the kind of memories that live forever in your bones. And just as I was connecting to that joy, another presence arrived, her grandmother. Her spirit came in like a calm wave, and with her help, I guided the woman into a meditation. It wasn't just about seeing visions, it was about cleansing her heart, clearing the emotional imbalance she didn't even realize she had been dragging behind her for too long. When she left, she was not the same. Something inside her had shifted, not fixed, not perfect, but lighter.

CELLAR SPIDER / DADDY LONG LEGS

-Take risks - you are lucky

-You have a force field to guard against negative energy or influences.

-You are an ancient soul, find balance between your physical and emotional self.

-Be mindful of your thoughts, feelings, and actions while developing self-confidence.

-You've been blessed with spiritual purity and innocence and a pure heart.

-You are constantly watched and surrounded with comporting energy, guardian angels, and spirit guides.

-Face your fears = Seek solutions rather than dwelling on your fears.

-Trust in yourself when making decisions, always make them in your best interests.

-Take leaps of faith towards your dreams. There is nothing to fear especially with your business and career.

-Don't lose faith in other people.

-Stop doubting yourself because of past mistakes.

-Meditate to harness wisdom.

-Always be on the lookout for new opportunities, this gives you an advantage over others.

-Your present lifetime is very rare, take advantage of it all.

#7

SHE WANTED CONTROL

Not every session begins with gratitude. Some people walk in dragging storms behind them. She was one of them. I don't even think she knew why she came to see me, maybe she was bored, maybe someone pushed her to it, maybe she thought I'd be another circus act with incense and cheap hope. But from the moment she sat down, it was clear, she hated everything. Her life, her people, this country. Her words were not just complaints; they were venomous. Spirit had already told me: Go deep. My feathers knew and they showed me that a deep spiritual cleanse was needed. The room shifted before I even burned my sage. When I prayed over her, I felt a heave energy trapped, like tangled webs up her left side and locked along her spine. She barely participated. Her energy was closed like a vault. I reached out to her ancestors, but they wouldn't come. No loved ones. No guides. No voices. Just silence. That's rare. When ancestors pull away, it means one thing, she wasn't ready. Not to heal. Not to listen. Not even to feel. Still, Spirit spoke. I gave her what she needed: a seven-day mirror exercise to break her self-loathing. Cold plunges to shock her nervous system back to presence. Night meditations to pull her into stillness. She kind of rolled her eyes as I spoke, and then I saw it.. She would not do it. Spirit showed me clearly that she would go back to the palm readers, the crystal ball gypsies, the ones who tell you what you want to hear instead of what your soul actually needs to hear. And that's okay.

Because healing is not forced. You must choose it. You have to want it more than you want your pain.

9 SPOTTED MOTH

-Beginning a period of transformation

-It is time to pay attention to your feelings, clarify your movement through them, and discern what is real and what is not.

*Discover the whys and you will be free of yourself.

-Be aware of that which you could be hiding from yourself. Be mindful, you are using your emotions to keep yourself protected from others.

-Now is the time you transform your emotional energy, move away from drama and into something closer to your heart. To do this you must have faith in your journey and trust that you will see the light even if things seem complicated now. Use your heart to guide you.

-Move towards the light and face your truths.

-Do not fear or avoid what you cannot see about yourself.

- You must know what light can harm and desire for something better.

-Seek deeper into your subconscious, that is where your true self lives.

*Remember your connection to perfection exists in your imagination and can never be fully achieved.

• Remember all the good you see in others is also in you. Do not forget!

•Be self-confident and accept yourself for who you really are.

*Use your spirit guide!

WORK/JOB: Counselor / advice giver, highly sought after friend

PRAY FOR: psychic awareness , body movement, mental clarity

THE JOURNEY BACK TO HER INNER CHILD

I had a client that came to me, and from the beginning I could feel her pain wasn't just about her current situation. She was going through a bitter separation, and her ex was trying to scare her, threatening her financially and threatening to take their daughter away. But as soon as I called in Spirit and began to pray, I saw straight into her soul. It was strong and soft. A rare combination that most people do not understand, let alone honor.

But then I saw her mind and her mind was broken, beaten, and scared. Not just by what was happening now, but by what she had been carrying her entire life.

Spirit showed me clearly what to do: I had to take her back to her childhood. The time when nobody protected her. The time when no one stood up for her. The time when her voice was silenced before it ever got a chance to form. I saw that a piece of her soul had been left behind. Alone, still waiting to be retrieved.

Through guided meditation and prayer, I asked Spirit to show her what she needed to see. I held space as we journeyed together, and when she finally met that little version of herself, she broke down and wept. And I wept with her. She found her. She embraced her. She gave her the love no one else ever had.

She found a part of her she thought was gone forever. And she walked out of that session not just lighter, but whole. Strong and soft like she was always meant to be.

Sometimes the transformation is not about fixing the present, it is about healing the past, so the present no longer controls you. That day, Spirit reminded me that not every woman comes in to find answers. Some come in to finally find themselves.

ASIAN LADY BUG

-You are blessed and have garnered significant attention due to your unique appearance.

-Rejoice in the fact that you embody the virtues of bravery and courage.

*Remember to face life's challenges with determination and resilience.

-You represent the interconnectedness of life and the beauty of diversity.

-You represent a unique blend of qualities and strengths.

-Embrace your individuality while fostering a sense of unity and harmony with the world around you.

-Face life's challenges head on and embrace the power living within yourself to overcome future obstacles.

-Remember you are protected by a higher power, a guardian angel, and the inverse itself.

-The representation of your physical appearance is associated with creativity, enthusiasm, passion, increased artistic expression, ingenuity, and inspiration.

*Respect and honor mother Earth and appreciate the beauty and interconnectedness of all living beings.

-Take all opportunities for personal growth knowing that positive circumstances are on the horizon.

*Focus on life's positives.

-You are always surrounded with love, commitment, and healthy relationships.

-Remember to nurture and cherish the meaningful connections in your life.

-Remember to embrace change and strive for the betterment of yourself and your circumstances.
-Leave worrying behind, happiness is on its way.
*Meditate

PRAY FOR: emotional balance and positive thinking

THE BEAUTY SHE COULDN'T SEE

She walked in with her head tilted slightly down, not in shame, but in a quiet sort of protection.
She was a young woman, barely stepping into life, but already worn from it. She had a cleft palate and years of carrying other people's stares, their comments, their silence.
 She did not come for magic or miracles. She came because she wanted to feel something. A shift. A moment. A little direction.
Her energy was fragile but powerful, like someone who has had to fight through the noise just to hear their own heartbeat. And that is what we did. My message was gentle, my voice was soft and almost quiet. And as I guided her into meditation, that undeniable softening that happens when someone finally gives themselves permission to exist, without shame, without apology happened. It was a reset.
A full-body, full-spirit, full-heart reset. During the entire session, she cried. Not the kind of tears that come from sadness, but the ones that mean relief. The kind that mean maybe, just maybe self-love is possible.
Sometimes the smallest spirits bring the loudest healing. And sometimes, healing starts with simply being seen.

DOVE

-Protection and guidance
-You have the power and resources needed to flourish in any situation in which you find yourself.
-Make sacrifices to get the things you desire the most.
-You should be willing to give up some things you enjoy to accomplish your goals in life.
→ Rid yourself of toxic emotions you have been harboring.
-Move forward
-Rely more on your intuition and less on your senses.
-You are worrying too much. Have faith that everything will be fine.
-Stop hiding your true self from others.
- Do not give up pursuing your dreams no matter how many obstacles.
-Tap into your spiritual journey as it will help with your personal power to explore the depths of "the unseen" world.
- Be patient but move steadily, move slowly with deliberateness
-Be mindful and vigilant even in times of change.
-Take a break from the monotony of everyday routines, make space for short but meaningful adventures.
-Reclaim your power!

PRAY FOR: Healing, renewal, fertility, dislike of being in the public eye
JOB / CALLING: Music, public speaking, excellent parent

SHE WASN'T EVEN AWARE OF HER OWN POWER

I had a client that came in to see me. She looked like someone used to doing everything on her own. Her presence was quiet and heavy. I noticed her eyes. Their power spoke to me without her knowing it was even there. They were eyes full of responsibility. Eyes that had seen too much and held too many people together. Before I even finished my opening prayer, two women came through strong, her mother and her grandmother. You could feel the power of their love fill the space. They came to lift her up, to remind her of the force she is. They spoke about things that no one else could have known. Secret struggles. Money stress. Sleepless nights. The feeling of carrying everything and still not doing enough. But they told her that her money was blessed and protected. That she did not need to worry so much, because things are already moving in her favor behind the scenes. They also brought up her son, told her he needed to get his hearing checked. That this was the real reason behind his school struggles and his speech delays. She froze. Tears welled up. Because deep down she knew something was off, but no one had connected the dots until now. Then came her daughter, the one she adopted with so much love. Holy Spirit spoke clearly though me about this child's needs, sensitivities, and her soul.

Spirit gave her answers she did not even know she was allowed to ask. Her mother and grandmother reminded her of her resilience and patience.

They praised her for constantly moving forward even

when the path is not clear. We did a deep limpia (cleanse) for healing and renewal.

I programed into her subconscious mind that she is a powerful mother, a quiet leader. A spiritual voice. And when she finally tapped into her own strength during the meditation,

you could feel the energy in the room. She didn't need to "learn" her power. She remembered it.

It was always there. She just needed to be reminded.

EUROPEAN HORNET

*Wake up and be true to yourself!

-Remember to take care of your energy and your vitality.

*Remember to appreciate and feel gratitude for your life's wonderful people, places, and experiences.

-Move with caution when moving forward.

- Reflect on your actions, certain choices are affecting more than just you. And you may be unaware of how you have affected some people and things in your life recently.

-Use your great ambition to achieve your goals.

- Community - work - aggression -use it to guide others - you can show them the importance of being kind and reflecting on their actions

- End of an era, conflict, or cycle

-It is time to let go and move on

-Control your impulses.

-Remember just thinking about your dreams will not make them come true as quickly as going out and doing it.

-Make a plan, work towards it, and let nothing get in your way.

*Ask for help when life feels out of control.

-Get your life in order, face up to its challenges and take action.

PRAY FOR: guidance, productivity, wisdom, will power
♡

I FACED THE WALL INSTEAD

There was a man who came to me for a reading. He did not walk in broken or in crisis. He came out of curiosity.

That is what he said. But I already knew he was coming. That morning something visited me during my chants, a spirit old ancient recycled. Not just someone's grandpa or cousin on the other side. This was something older. Something that has been walking the Earth for centuries.

I do not know what it was, but it came close to me and whispered, "Prepare yourself and show respect." I prepared my space with slow meticulous chants and as I did, I could feel something sacred was about to happen. When he came in, I could not face him. Literally, my body turned away from him on its own. I sat with my back to him, I could not explain it, it just had to be that way. I spoke and he listened.

The reading went by quickly. It did not feel bad, but it did not feel big either. It was quiet and still, like talking into the wind. Like doing a ceremony and wondering if anything landed. He left very polite with no emotions on his face, no questions, just thank you and gone. I still think about it, not in a dramatic way but like a whisper that follows me sometimes. What was that? Who was that?

 Why was I told to prepare with such care only for the moment to pass like nothing? Maybe it was not about the reading.

Maybe it was not even about him.

Maybe that soul was just stopping by to remember what it feels like to sit in a room with reverence.

Maybe I was the one being tested to honor something I couldn't understand.

We don't always get the answers. Not right away. Not in this lifetime. But I believe in soul memory. I believe there is a reason I turned my back.

Maybe I was bowing without knowing it, maybe Spirit just needed one last goodbye in a human body before moving on. I'll find out one day, not now, but later. After this life when all the veils are gone, and I remember everything I once knew before being born.

CRANEFLY

-This present period of your life is time to give your best effort to achieve success, show the world what you can do.

-Change in your life is needed.

-Seek the knowledge of astral travel and new knowledge.

-Find balance between love, life, and independence.

-Your voice needs to be used uniquely.

*Remember despite your delicate appearance, you are a strong survivor!

-Remember to approach situations with others who are vulnerable with care and empathy.

- Keep pushing forward even through challenges, know that changes are coming, and you will adapt to new circumstances.

-It is time to break free of old patterns that are holding you back.

- Remember to approach life with an open heart and mind free of judgement or preconceptions.

-Do not continue to hide in a safe environment, where the light is switched on.

-Know that you will always be safe when you are following your purpose.

-Lost in choices - if you know deep down that you are settling for less than your higher purpose, what good does that do for you?

-Use your life to put light into the world, in your own unique way. Everything that inspires you will inspire others.

-When the world around you makes you believe it is hard, it is time to spread your wings and fly in complete freedom. Believe in yourself.

-You will be an example to others on a global scale.

<u>BLOCKS AND CLEANSE</u>
Logic, reasoning, creativity, balance, contemplation, stability, imagination

WEAR: indigo
EAT: purple diet
CHANT: OMMM
What spirit animal told me my client was suffering from: Headaches, eyes / vision, sinus, hearing, dizzy spells, pain

THE FLIGHT BEYOND THE BODY

He walked in tall; he was one of the tallest men I've seen. Shoulders wide. Strong like he had built entire cities with his being. The kind of man people stare at when he passes. But Spirit does not care about appearances. Spirit only cares about what you hide behind them. Before he even got to my door, I was already in prayer. And during that prayer, I heard very clearly, this one needs to rest. Not just rest like sleep. This soul needed to leave the planet for a while to get real rest, the kind not found on Earth. He needs a trip to another realm where the noise stops, and truth is all that is left. But here's the thing, I had never done that before. Not fully. Not like that. I had no map, no manual, no plan. Spirit whispered, "You don't need one." He sat down. I gave him his spirit animal reading. He didn't flinch when I told him. He didn't laugh either.

Just nodded, quietly. I knew right away this wasn't a typical reading. There wasn't going to be a bunch of questions.

There was not going to be a flood of tears. This was not about healing the past. This was about launching the soul forward and out of the body. I put my hands on his chest and whispered words that didn't come from me, they came through me. I don't remember all of them. I just remember the moment he dropped. Not fainted. Not fell asleep. But he left, his body stayed but he was no longer in the room. Eyes closed, breathing steady, lips gently parted. That man went so deep into meditation that I felt like his body was floating. I stayed focused on the sound of my voice, prayed, then spoke to his subconscious. I told his soul it was time to rest, time to reset, time to remember who he really is, time to let go of the noise, the demands, the armor. Then I gently brought him back. He opened his eyes slowly, like a man waking up from another life. He didn't say much. Just hugged me in silence. It was all understood. After he left, I collapsed. My body could not hold the energy anymore. I laid on the couch, wide-eyed, vibrating, but peaceful. It was unbelievable to me how someone so gigantic could "float" in meditation. It felt like I had opened a door to something I didn't fully understand yet. But I trusted Spirit. This was also the first time I got actual tools like foods, colors, chants to give to my clients as homework. Simple things that would restore balance to their mind and body after they leave my space. Because the truth is, a reading is just the beginning it's not the medicine. They are.

BLUE BETTLE

-You have been granted renewed strength, determination, and resilience

*Time for your clan/tribe has come. Know that you will be helped with your network and people will bond with you to achieve your goals.

->You are chosen to clean up our world. By cleansing and purification of minds and belief patterns.

*Remember one person's trash is another person's treasure.

*You are part of an order of Cleopatra with knowledge of the oldest regions of the Earth.

-You have great camouflage to fool predators- know when to take yourself out of the limelight.

*Air and water = new alignment

      -Air = higher thinking, communicating with angels, spirits, sensitivity, clairvoyancy, and greater vision

      -Water = grounding, stability, trust, material realm, safe, consistent

-Great deal of change

-Stand true to yourself.

*Regroup – Return to your community of heart to find peace and understanding.

*Pay attention – socially – expand your senses to the spiritual level and walk with awareness in your heart.

*Strive for positivity and the effective use of your time and energy.

*Look to the sky – freedom

*Jupiter

*You are larger than life -there's a better life ahead.

-You need to think and live bigger.
PRAY FOR: Renewal, safety, restoration, mind, body, spirit, smell

THE CHASE

She came in quiet but full of chaos underneath. I know because I could feel it in my stomach. She had been trying too hard for too long, carrying too much, chasing something that always moved just a few steps ahead. She had just come back from the chase. Movie stars. Big names. Bigger promises. None of it had stuck. Everything she thought was going to happen fell apart. And what hurt her most was that it all looked so good. But behind the scenes, it was cold. It was fake. It was cruel. And it was expensive. Financially. Emotionally. Spiritually. She was questioning everything.

I knew before she opened her mouth that this wasn't going to be about what went wrong. It was going to be about who she forgot she was. Spirit brought in the Blue Beetle. It showed up with strength, ancient, sacred, and royal. Not loud, but undeniable. Spirit spoke though me, you are not meant to just survive in this world. You were sent to help clean it.

Not with bleach or fists but with truth. With light. With remembering.

With showing people how to turn trash into treasure. It reminded her that she came from old lineages. That her beauty wasn't just her face, it was her mind, her presence, her ability to endure and still love. She didn't need more spotlight, she needed more alignment. Her job now was to camouflage, reconnect, and rebuild her foundation.

Her father came through too. Just stood behind her. Said nothing at first. Just held her in love. His presence alone was medicine. It grounded her.

She had been trying to make herself smaller to fit the room. But the room was never meant to hold her. We didn't finish the session with big answers or rituals. We finished in stillness. I watched her energy shift and her breath came back. Her spine straightened. Her voice was softer but stronger.

She said, "I feel like I can think clearly again." Spirit didn't tell her what to do. Spirit reminded her what she's capable of. And when she left, she didn't rush to post it or prove it. She just left steady.

And I knew she'd be okay.

Because Blue Beetle only shows up for the ones who are finally ready to live like they were always meant to.

ASIAN CRICKET

-Your gut feelings are telling you something, trust them!

-The things you have been dreaming about and working for are now possible.

*Stay open to guidance and messages so that you will know what to do.

→ You may be guided to buy a lottery ticket or interview for a new job- do it knowing you are at the right place and the right time.

*All things are possible right now! All you have to do is feel like you deserve it!

-Use the power of your voice to attract what you want in life. Remember you are an excellent communicator.

-Use music to heal yourself.

-Change direction.

-Call on your spirit guide during this time of transformation, you will get help finding your soul song and the power to speak your truth with conviction.

-Stop swallowing your words.

-Get ready for your new awakening after you use your intuition and voice.

-Stay grounded. Keep your head, heart, and spirit in symmetry.

-Be sure that your desire to be successful and get what you want in life does not cause others harm or worse, irreparable damage.

-You have the power to move large groups of people with your energetic force.

*We have given you a sign, when you become quite = something is wrong =check your environment

***Luck

Higher consciousness and presence of mind, focus, prosperity

THE AWAKENING THAT NEVER HAPPENED

She came to me with a curious grin, designer clothes, jewelry, bag, and an expensive coat. From the outside, she glowed, perfect skin, perfect teeth, perfect posture. She was polished, powerful, and full of what some would call life, but I've learned to call that particular shine something else, distraction. She was a doctor, a woman of logic and white lab coats, trained to trust data and dismiss dreams. She came not out of desperation, but out of intrigue. Maybe even Skepticism. I was new in her country. New always pulls people in. When I gave her the message, she sat like stone. Eyes polite. Lips frozen in a smile so practiced it almost made me forget what I was seeing beneath it all. Her energy turned cold, resistant. The block she threw up the moment Spirit began to speak hit me like a gust of sterile wind. The kind you only find in hospitals. Clean, quiet, but lifeless. Spirit told me to guide her into meditation to stop her mind from sprinting into next week's appointments and bring her soul back to this exact moment. I tried. I really did. I prayed over her, whispered blessings over the tight muscles she wouldn't let relax. But her body laid there stiff, tense, like she was afraid to fall too deep. She never gave herself permission to rest. Even in stillness, she resisted.

When she left, she thanked me kindly, the way people thank a barista for an oat milk latte. Like nothing happened. Like Spirit hadn't just tried to save her. But Spirit doesn't forget.

Every so often, when I see her pop up on my feed, smiling in another city, speaking at another conference, healing others with medicine while quietly avoiding her own, I feel a tug. A silent invitation to pray for her again. And I do. Not because she asked. Not because I think I can fix her. But because I hope one day she allows herself to be both, brilliant and broken, human and healer, science and Spirit.

VIPER SNAKE

-Transformation is now in progress you will be shedding old skin and emotions and transforming them into something bigger and better.

-There is someone in your inner circle of friends and family that you cannot trust. Watch for signs - signs of hypocrisy, slander, and maliciousness. When you spot them, refuse to engage in their nasty games.

-Be careful with your words and actions, learn to control your temper.

-Remember stay focused and true to yourself.

-With change and new beginnings remember that you are a survivor, wise and powerful. Don't be afraid change is necessary.

*Find Healing in Kundalini energy for problems in the base of your spine.

-Shed your old self.

*Temptation

-Fertility and growth -creative life force

*Remember you are highly protected

-You are a sexual being; embrace it, enjoy it, explore it, know it is safe for you to do so.

-Stay connected to your true self.

-Remember you have the natural ability to balance energy, use your hands as a gifted healer.

CLEANSE FOR: Patience, creativity, wisdom, balance

SHEDDING SHAME, EMBRACING POWER

He was a beautiful man. Well put together, smelled magnificent, muscular, and magnetic. But I could see it, behind his charm, Spirit showed me venom in his circle.

Women close to him, maybe sisters or cousins, feeding doubt and shame into his friendships. Slandering him. Whispering things they wouldn't dare say to his face. As we began the session, Spirit was loud and clear: tell him not to be ashamed of his work. What he did was consensual, adult, and clean, free of drugs and abuse. And at the end of the day, it was work. I told him that. He breathed out like a man finally allowed to be himself.

Then he told me what he did for a living. And I felt that flicker of surprise, only because of how much the world trains us to judge what doesn't fit into neat boxes. But Spirit reminded me, immediately, that God does not look with judgment. Only humans do. And often the ones shouting from the pulpits are hiding filth far worse than any man living in truth.

The viper snake had come to walk beside him. Transformation. Shedding old shame. Embracing his sexuality and power, not as a curse, but as a gift. He was protected, Spirit said. I still pray that he never dims himself to comfort small minds. Because what he carries is sacred, and the world needs more people unafraid to be fully, unapologetically themselves.

SNAIL

-Home

-Slow down you have been spending so much time focusing on goals that you've missed something, let go for a moment so that you will be able to see it.

- Be sure to trust your process, what may seem like forever is just a small moment.

- Release your beliefs about not getting things done on time.

-Do not cause yourself added stress.

- Use your time wisely knowing that you do not have time for everything.

-Divide your priorities and set up allocated time to create.

*Time Management

-Remain in the present moment.

-Rely on instinct, intuition, and patience.

-Take your time making decisions.

-Remember challenges will bring you growth and transformation.

-Meditate find stillness to quiet the mind.

CLEANSE FOR: Balance, trust, emotional issues

SLOW DOWN, IT'S ALREADY YOURS

I sat in meditation waiting for her, she was late. Very late, usually I cancel if someone is more than ten minutes late. Mainly because it takes so much energy to wait and stay connected. But her spirit animal reading was all about time. So, I waited. My client arrived, breathing heavily, on the verge of tears, and wanting to use the restroom. She fussed with her phone and finally came into my sacred space. She came in looking tired, like many do. Her energy was scattered, her eyes jumping from one thought to the next even as she sat still.

I was able to look into her soul and saw that she had been chasing something for so long that she could not even remember why she wanted it in the first place. A dream job? A new house? The perfect version of herself? She had become addicted to motion, to productivity, to the feeling of checking off boxes. But in the process, she had lost her peace.

The Snail came to her gently, reminding her that not everything worth having comes fast or loud. This was about home. Coming back to her body, her spirit, her heart. Spirit said she was not late. Not behind. Not failing. She just needed to stop long enough to see that what she was looking for had been quietly waiting all along. I gave her her message and guided her into meditation, where for the first time in a long time, she allowed herself to do nothing. To breathe. To trust. And in that stillness, she cried.

Sometimes we forget that rushing is not the same as progress. The Snail shows us that sacred things unfold slowly. With patience. And with grace.

EUROPEAN BLACK BIRD

-Only by admitting your true feelings to yourself right now can you move forward with love and respect for yourself.

-Reach higher.

-Continue to strive for excellence in all you do.

-Set bigger goals.

-Be mindful you are becoming too territorial. There is a need for you to let others into your space.

-Find your voice and form your own personality, express yourself uniquely.

-Speak the truth to those you love even when it hurts.

-Remember to appreciate nature.

-Remember to protect your family with all you've got.

-Honor your insatiable hunger for all kinds of knowledge.

-Remember you are a natural leader and an inspiration to those around you with your actions and lifestyle.

-Do not over analyze you can become over domineering

CLEANSE FOR: fear, gentleness, ferocity, love, speaking / voice, wisdom

THE SONG SHE REFUSED TO HEAR

I had a client that booked an online session with me, and from the very start, Spirit did not waste time. I was allowed to leave my body and float out of my body in California and into her European villa. Through remote viewing, I saw everything: her marriage held together by threads of routine, guilt, and reputation. It was already gone, but no one had said it aloud yet.

Spirit showed me her husband's mind. He was no longer in love, hadn't been in years. He stayed only for the comfort of the known, for the adult children he didn't want to hurt, and for the financial fallout that a divorce would bring. Not for her. Not because he still desired the life they built together.

I delivered Spirit's message gently but firmly. She needed to stop focusing on controlling him and instead begin healing herself. He would stay, if he saw her fall in love with herself, her life, they life he had worked so hard to provide for her to be happy in. He would stay if he saw her happy. Spirit showed me that there was a path of peace available, but it required letting go with grace, not clinging with fear.

But I could hear it in her voice, I could feel a toxicity in her sounds when she spoke. I still remember how it made my ear feel. She did not want peace. She wanted control. She wanted spells. Hexes. Manipulation.

Anything to keep him in the house even if his heart had already left it. She did not understand that the European Blackbird sings a song of truth, not force. This bird teaches us to admit our deepest feelings and move forward in self-respect, to speak painful truths with clarity, not desperation.

Months later, I felt her again. That is what happens with some readings, they stay with me. Her energy reached out in grief. He had left. Just like Spirit warned, her domineering behavior had pushed him away completely. And still, she searched for someone to curse, something to blame.

But love cannot be forced. And black magic only darkens the one who casts it.

I pray for her still. Not for him to come back, but for her to wake up to her own soul song. To stop shouting and finally start listening to herself, to Spirit, and to the healing silence she's been avoiding for years.

BLUE BUTTERFLY

-Major transformations are taking place right now with the outcome being different than what you expected.

-Remember to embrace changes in your environment and within your emotional body.

- This physical transformation of energy around you is taking root in ways that will surprise you.

-Release any expectations you may have about the outcome of this change. Do not try to control any of it, go with the flow.

- Get up, move, dance, karate, work out. Move physically to remain mentally fit.

-Trust yourself, embrace your own journey, and tap into your inner strength.

-Renewal Period

- Spirituality-dig deep

*Remember to have open and honest communication, especially with matters of the heart.

-You are protected – Creativity, inspiration, and artistic expression

-Seek Inner Wisdom.

-Keep your heart open, your angels are trying to reach you, ask them for guidance and protection.

- Stay hopeful, seek calmness, peace, and tranquility.

-Approach life with a sense of adventure.

-Don't forget to appreciate the little moments that might get you closer to your spiritual self.

*Throat Chakra = open communication and self-expression

CLEANSE FOR: mental clarity, soul journey, intuition, personal growth

HIDDEN AGENDAS

He came into our lives smiling, eager, full of compliments and helpful hands. Young, ambitious, and curious. Said he wanted to volunteer, help us with social media, offer his time, learn from us. He quickly began to cling, to ask for things, and yet I saw the sparkle in his eyes. He asked for a reading and in his session, Spirit showed me a bit of his intentions.
Not evil. Just calculating. A social climber, quietly playing chess while pretending he was still learning checkers. Still, I welcomed him. Why? Because sometimes even butterflies begin as something messy. Spirit told me: let him come. He was useful to the brand at that moment in time.
Later, the mask dropped. His intentions surfaced. He was not in our lives out of devotion, but for access. Exposure. Status. And that's okay. It hurt a little, but it taught us a lot. Not every person sent into your life is meant to stay. Some arrive to test your instincts. Others are mirrors showing you what you no longer need to carry. When I think of him, I wish him and his family well. I thank the experience and release it with love. I hope he learned something.

WASP

-Go work on your goals and your goals will work on you because of all the good things we build end up building us.

• Make a plan! Just thinking about your dreams won't make them come true-go after them!

-Don't let anything get in your way.

-Apply your passion to the reality you want to achieve.

-Remember resistance to change is self-sabotage.

-Allow yourself to believe again, that all things are possibles, and that you deserve to have all your dreams come true.

* Relationship

-Tap into your inner creativity.

-Communication

-Think outside the box and take on new projects. Find innovative solutions to problems.

-Remember communicate honestly and openly with others.

-Let go of old ways and embrace new beginnings.

* It is time to trust that whatever you decide to do will lead you somewhere even better than where you currently are.

-Listen the universe is trying to get you to connect more with your divine femininity.

-Remember to connect to the softer, slower, and more creative side of yourself.

- Remain flexible. There will always be solutions. Stay creative and keep your eyes open.

-Organize yourself.

CLEANSE FOR: Held back feelings, words, self-care, emotions

SACRED SPACES AND SILENT DESIRES

She came because her influencer friend did. I could feel it instantly; this was not about Spirit at first. It was about curiosity, status, maybe even entertainment. But Spirit does not care why you show up. If you knock on the door, it will always open.

As soon as I connected, visions came flooding in. Not loud or dramatic, but quiet, intricate like puzzle pieces. Flashes of her life, not the one she presented, but the real one. A deep love lost. A devotion to her children that ran like roots in the earth. But beneath it all... a whisper. A hidden longing. She wanted something sacred that belonged only to her.

She didn't say it out loud. I am not sure she even fully knew it herself at the time.

But Spirit did. Her soul was sweet and gentle, even if her path was a labyrinth. Time passed and I saw that she had opened her own sacred place. A quiet fire inside her finally took form. It made me smile. Not because I needed recognition, but because her spirit had followed the thread. Maybe she remembered the reading, maybe not. But that seed Spirit planted had grown.

RED ADMIRAL BUTTERFLY

-Embrace change-new beginnings

- It is time for a spiritual awakening.

-Have hope remember you are blessed with guiding and supporting angels, call on them for help.

-Begin to celebrate life with your creativity and self-expression.

-Remember to remain balanced.

*Release expectations and control of:

    -Marriage Love

    -ying / yang

    -major changes

*It is time to let go of what's holding you back.

-Remember there is no light without darkness, no evil without good, no happy without sadness. It is only when we accept all of these contrasts that we find peace and harmony.

*Trust your intuition.

-Begin to record your ideas to awaken your creativity.

? Relationship question - Can you make this relationship healthy or not?

-Have faith in your emotional capacity to heal.

- It is time to get out of protective cocoon.

-Be ready to expand your family, or social circle in a fun and lively way.

*Pay attention to your intuition in financial decisions. Remember fortune favors the bold!

BLOCKS AND CLEANSE
Sacral Chakra
EAT: More Orange foods
REPEAT: Centering Affirmations

DO: Stimulate your creativity, Journal

DRINK: ginger tea, licorice, mints, cinnamon vanilla, hibiscus teas

THE SESSION THAT FELT EMPTY

I had a client come to me, a big TV producer. You'd probably know her name if I said it. She came not because she needed help but out of curiosity. Like she wanted to prove something to herself. Or maybe to Spirit. She sat silent the entire time. She didn't cry. She didn't nod. She didn't ask questions. But her stillness wasn't disbelief. I could read her brain. She believed every word I said, she just did not have the capability to express emotion. Her body didn't know how. Years in survival mode had made her sharp and polished on the outside but numb inside. It wasn't her fault. That was just how she had learned to survive. So, the session felt empty. Like I was pouring clean water into a tightly sealed jar. Nothing landed. But Spirit told me: "Nothing is wasted. Something moved." And I know that to be true. Some people don't show it, but their soul is listening. Sometimes the most powerful awakenings are the quietest. Sometimes all you can do is plant the seed, water the soil with intention, and walk away. Because it is not about the reaction. It's about what grows after. Maybe one day she'll sit down with a notebook and the words will pour out. Maybe she'll drink a tea I recommended and feel her sacral center finally flicker back on. Or maybe she'll just feel something. Some sessions don't end in tears. They end in silence. But silence has a vibration too. One only Spirit can hear.

HYENA

- Your words are important; they are also valuable to others. Speak up!
-Remember you are now in a more social phase in your life.
-Spirit insists that you communicate with those around you more openly and honestly.
-Choose the words you use very carefully.
-You are placed to build up those around you and help them grow.
*Focus more on family - give them 2 weeks of undivided attention this action will strengthen bonds and build confidence.
*Remember you must participate in your community. Withdrawal is not an option. Find ways to participate progressively and in a healthy way.
-Embrace the feminine energy within you required to find balance. For far too long you have given up part of yourself to opposing forces. Leadership requires balance in all areas.
-You must take on male and female energies to bring about compromise.
*Continue to live by your instinct and intuition.
-Use comic relief to lighten the mood in uncomfortable situations.
*Face your fear of nervousness involving yourself in your community. Call on your spirit guides in all meetings or conversations for social acceptance.

THE POWER BEHIND THE SMILE
I had a session with a woman who many would call powerful. She walked in like a storm wearing heels,

shoulders straight, presence sharp. She founded a medical center in a country where having a non-profit is like riding a unicorn to work. She held recognition trophies in countless social circles. People listened when she spoke, they gave when she took and donated even more when she took and took again.But when Spirit showed her to me, I did not see her résumé. I saw her spirit. She was a taker, yes, but not because she meant harm. She used it to help. She was just someone who had been surviving too long on control and perception. Underneath her demands, her status, her "perfect public self" there was just a woman who wanted to feel. Who did not know how. I saw it. Spirit showed me that she had not yet found her balance, she had pushed away her feminine softness to rise in a world that only valued her masculine power. But both were needed. Spirit made that very clear. Leadership is nothing without heart. Without community. Without softness. The lesson wasn't easy. She didn't cry. But something in her shifted. The smile at the end of our session. It didn't try so hard to be seen. It just was. Sometimes people don't change right away. But sometimes, a reading cracks something open. I hope she did not go back to her old ways. I pray she gave her family those two weeks of undivided attention Spirit asked for. That she let people in. That she learned the strength in receiving, not taking. Because when Spirit asks us to speak t's not just for power. It's to connect. It's to tell the truth. It's to lead with others, not just in front of them.

WHITE BUTTERFLY

-It is your responsibility to make your own way in life with faith, accept the changes as they come.

-Massive transformation

-Embrace changes is your environment with your emotional body.

-Do not try to control changes.

*Move

-Long soul journey

*Explore your own psychic abilities.

*Know that the soul of a dearly departed on is always with you.

-Keep your faith

PRAY FOR: Purity, innocence, spirituality, protection

THE VISITOR WITH WINGS

The spirit animal message was short. The session was virtual. My client was small and quiet. But sometimes the quiet ones carry the most weight. Before I got into it, I smelled the scent of sugar and a cotton apron. I closed my eyes and saw the aprons that go all the way to the top and cover your chest. I also saw embroidered doilies. Then with a gentle squeeze on my shoulders, her grandma came through. She told her she was the white butterfly in her life. Every single time, that was her! My client nodded, then, unexpectedly, a male friend, her best friend, stepped forward, with this confident ease. He joked around about memories of sacred moments they shared together. But he did not come alone he brought her mother. At that moment, everything changed.

She whispered through me that she saw her life unraveling in a beautiful way. Not falling apart but unfolding. And with it, her own spiritual gifts waking up. Like she's always had them, but buried them in logic and responsibility. Then she said it was time. Time to explore her own sight. Her own voice. Her own path. They wanted her to know they are with her. That the souls she lost aren't gone, they're her guardians now. They walk with her. That friend? He still talks to her. The butterfly? That is her grandmother reminding her to breathe and believe again.

Sometimes a session does not need many words. Just presence. Just confirmation that you are not alone in this world or the next.

She left the reading lighter. I could feel her spirit stretch. A quiet kind of peace. Somewhere out there, she saw a white butterfly that week, I just know it!

BLACK SPIDER

-Something you have been working on has flourished, congratulations!

-Creativity is at its peak!

-Embrace your ideas and dreams and take action.

-You must take the time to find a balance between your past and your future.

-Remember your reality is yours to create.

-It is time to reevaluate what you are doing, there is something that you are creating that is not in line with the dreams you are trying to create. Take inventory of your thoughts and see where you are sabotaging yourself.

- Pay close attention to your intuition and your inner knowledge, adjust accordingly.

* Remember you are blessed with the ability to balance the past and future, physical and spiritual, male and female.

-Use your creativity to write – story telling

CLEANSE FOR: balance, vibrational energy, grudges or feeling vengeful, family bonds and complications

What spirit animal told me my client was suffering from: stress, anxiety, pressure, feeling trapped in past trauma

THREAD BY THREAD

It was a virtual reading. A young girl, early twenties maybe. Her energy was clean but heavy. She came seeking direction with love, life, career the usual when everything feels like it's slipping out of your hands. She had just lost her job and broke up with her boyfriend.

She had moved back in with her parents. Her light had dimmed. You could feel the fog around her. But spirit showed me something clear as day, her hair. I asked her, "Did you dye your hair last night?" She gasped. "Yes."

She had colored it dark, maybe hoping to match her mood or disappear in the mess. But spirit told her: "Change it back."

Not just the color, but the energy. She was trying to become someone that did not align with her dreams. That little act of coloring her hair was the first stitch in a pattern of self-sabotage.

Spirit reminded her: "Your creativity is your power. Use it." Write. Dream. Story tell. Shape your next chapter with conscious hands. She did not need a miracle. She just needed alignment. She needed to believe that the life she is imagining is already waiting, but she must build the bridge with action and truth.

She left with homework to write her story, not from the place she's in, but from the place she wants to be. Start with one small change. Like changing her hair back. Like forgiving herself.

We are all just webs, thread by thread, choice by choice, thought by thought.

STORK

- Spiritual Renewal / Remain grateful
-New beginnings
-You or someone close to you will become a parent.
-It is time for you to venture into new and unfamiliar territories.
-Stop letting fear hold you back.
*Remember to remain calm and collected.
-Watch what you say and keep your plans secret.
-Partner- remain faithful
* Protect your loved ones and place family above all things.
→ Great parent
*Express yourself through creative writing and other art forms.
→ Purification
→Water
*Long life
*Very lucky

DISCUSS: Family, balance, life cycles

WHEN THE TIME IS RIGHT

I had a session with a kind woman. She was the kind of woman who does not cry in front of strangers, even when her soul is screaming. After her I read the "baby part" of the spirit animal message, she asked me if I could see children in her future. But before spirit could even answer that, I was pulled somewhere else. They showed me her partner. The tension between them. Unspoken words sitting like heavy fog in their home. I felt it in her body, the way she carried love like a burden.

Not because she didn't want it, but because she didn't know where to place it anymore. I told her I needed to cleanse her first.

And him too, remotely, through prayer.

After the cleanse, something shifted. Not with tears or emotion, she didn't show much.

But her face softened. The weight eased. That is when spirit allowed me to see her daughter, not born yet, but waiting. Waiting for space. Waiting for peace. Waiting for her mother to choose love without fear. I didn't say it dramatically. I just told her gently, "Yes. There is a child. A daughter. When the time is right." She nodded once. Still holding it all in. But I saw it land. I saw her spirit listen. I pray she gets everything she's brave enough to admit she wants.

SQUIRREL

-You reap what you sow-take care in choosing the seeds you are planting.

-Have more fun - remember play is essential too do not be too busy taking life so seriously.

-Remember prepare for the future, retirement, insurance, simple preparations.

-Lighten your load of unnecessary things -past things that clutter your life right now and no longer serve you.

-Take time and listen to your inner self and focus on one thing at a time.

*Remain flexible and adaptable to all situations.

*Find harmony in your physical, emotional, and spiritual life.

-Remember be resourceful and make the most of what you have.

> Opportunities = act quickly and effectively.

→Balance work, play and rest.

→Socialize – it is important for you to interact with others.

-Embrace your inner curiosity and joy.

*Focus more on your desires and manifest them.

*Remember be present in the moment, fully immersing yourself in the here and now.

CLEANSE FOR: liveliness, playfulness, resourcefulness, adaptability, mindfulness, balance, proactive / preparation, socialization, fertility

THE FARM IN OREGON

She came into the room with a heaviness she couldn't quite name, something in between confusion and quiet desperation. On paper, she had already left him. But in real life, the two still lived under the same roof, shared the same bed more often than she'd admit, and split everything right down the middle, except clarity. She told me she wanted out. She just couldn't find the door. Her voice was soft, but her soul was screaming for direction. Spirit came in quickly, without hesitation. It didn't show me an argument, or an end marked by drama. Instead, I saw movement lateral movement. Oregon. A change so big it would shake the dust off her soul and allow her to breathe again. There, I saw a different kind of life waiting for her. Green. Earthy. Peaceful. And beside her, a man with quiet strength, his name was Eric. His energy didn't pull or push her. It simply made space. I told her everything exactly as I saw it, not to convince her, but because I knew it was already alive inside her. She just needed someone to name it. When I said his name, she went still. That kind of stillness that only happens when something resonates deep. Her eyes didn't fill with tears. They filled with recognition. She wasn't broken. She was in between lives. I did a cleanse for her. The weight she carried was not just her ex, it was years of habit, of responsibility, of making herself smaller so others could feel comfortable. I reminded her that the life she wanted, the one with more play, more space, more breath, wasn't a fantasy. It was preparation. A seed she had planted long ago. I still wonder if she went. If she packed up the pieces of her old life and headed toward something softer. I wonder if Eric really grows tomatoes or if it was just symbolic.

GOAT MOTH

- Pay attention to the signs you are receiving; it may be that you need to adjust your course.
- Be mindful of the fact that you are using your emotions to keep yourself protected from others.
-Have faith and trust your path.
*Know that you can go through these difficult times and go where others will not.
*Know that hard times will come to an ease.
-Great deal of transformation endings (death or ending)
-Remember to embrace your personality, do not hide from who you really are.
→Change-evaluate your routines and keep your passion alive, do not let anything keep you from living your dream.
-Let everything you do on a daily basis fascinate you. Be amazed in nature, in being you, being a mom. Find happiness in the small moments.
- Do not have certain secrets that you hold on to.
-There is no need to hold on to things that don't add any value, or to hold on to secrets that stress you. If they feel burdensome, discard them.
> Use your emotional energy to move away from drama.
-WORK: Peace and advice giving (counselor /advisor)
→ Work on your intuition and very own psychic awareness.

CLEANSE FOR: Emotional energy, self-love, self-esteem

PERMISSION TO HEAL

When she walked in, I could see her smile and scared look on her face. I've seen that look before. It is the face of someone who's mastered the art of survival but has forgotten what thriving feels like. We didn't get far into the reading before Spirit pulled something sharp from the quiet: a secret.

It sat heavy in her chest. She admitted to a love affair years ago, something that came and went like wildfire. It had been over for a long time, but it still haunted her. Especially now, in the colder seasons of her marriage. She did not miss him as much as she missed how she felt in that version of herself: alive, seen, desired. But the more she clung to the memory, the sicker she became. Literally.

Her skin broke out. Her stomach ached. She stress-ate to feel something, anything, other than invisible. And then she blamed her body for reacting, like it was betraying her. But it wasn't. It was crying out to be heard. Spirit let me see the man. His business. His children. His wife. He had moved on. She hadn't.

That's when I told her the truth: the love was real then, but it wasn't real now. And it was okay. It was over, and it had to be. I told her the past was not meant to be her punishment. It was meant to be her lesson. We did the cleanse together, pulling grief out of the layers where she had hidden it, not just from the world but from herself.

She wept not from heartbreak, but from release. The kind of release that comes when you realize you do not need anyone else to give you permission to heal. She didn't need to erase her past. She just needed to stop letting it define her future. I wonder if she has learned to laugh a little louder now. If she is eating food that loves her back. If her husband has started noticing her again or maybe, more importantly, if she has.

WHITE DOVE

- Slow down, pause and breath, know that you are surrounded by peace, love, purity, and divine intervention.
-Have hope in new beginnings.
-Prepare for a period of calm and balance in your life or an end to conflicts and disputes.
-Continue the process of spiritual cleansing and purification in your life.
-Prepare for a new romantic love -> analyze your old habits and take accountability of your old actions, remember to love first!
*Remember you are being guided by a higher power.
- Strive for peace in your life!
-Holy Spirit is present in your life bringing peace and forgiveness.
* Center yourself you will know what to do and what not to do, when the time comes, go with the flow!
-Faith- you must surrender
-Let go of what surrounds you and take time to find peace within you.
-Remember most chaos happens before your dreams come true.
* Remember to purify your thoughts!
-You are still attracting what you don't want in your life by focusing on it.
*New romance. New beginnings. New friendships.

THE SILENCE OF THE WHITE DOVE

She walked in holding herself together like a porcelain vase, intact, but only barely. Her voice was calm, but her energy screamed grief. Most people assume grief is loud, wailing, sobbing, undone. But sometimes it is silent, slow, and disguised as survival. I know it far too well, having worn it myself for the majority of my life. She said she wanted a reading to connect with loved ones on the other side. But within minutes, I knew she was not mourning the dead. She was mourning herself. The woman she used to be. Her husband had left her not long ago, slowly walked out after decades of being "the man beside her." And her adult children? Distant. No calls. No warmth.

No mother-to-mother intimacy. She was not just grieving the roles she had lost as a wife, mom, partner. She was grieving the purpose that had kept her alive for so many years. Now that it was gone, the silence of her days became unbearable. But what I recognized the most was not her sadness. It was her resistance to feeling it. She was still clinging to a mask of strength, still afraid that falling apart might mean she would never get back up.

The Holy Spirit entered the room before I even called it in. That is how I knew she wasn't alone, even if she felt like she was. I asked her to lie down on my treatment table. I placed my hands gently over her chest and forehead, and I let the energy do the work. I sang; I sang for both of us.

I used the memories of how I felt when my disguise melted away to melt hers with my melody. What poured out of her was not dramatic, it was sacred. Silent tears, a breath that finally slowed, and the faintest whisper of "I'm ok." She left with no makeup, no tears, no armor.

Just a softness in her eyes that had not been there before. She did not need predictions. She needed to be witnessed and held. And reminded that she had not disappeared.

The White Dove does not shout. It arrives in stillness. It waits on your windowsill until you are ready to open the curtains and see that peace was always within reach if you'd just let yourself stop running.

GRASSHOPPER

-You need to fully commit yourself to your decision, it's the only way to succeed with this venture at this time.

- Take the leap of faith - just do it, go for it.

-Adjustment: relationship, career, transition within

-Remember to use your instincts to capture the exact moment that will be most beneficial.

-Period of good luck, prosperity, renewal, and regeneration begins

-Remember to stay in the present moment.

- Use your unique and colorful appearance, creativity, and originality to think outside the box

*New beginnings!

+ love story / mom story

-Remember to connect with nature.

-Old family member or new friend will enter your life.

-Be proud of who you are and what you have accomplished. Show it off!

-Now is the best time to let go of the past!

- Remember every love story is different and may be best to give second chances and not let personal insecurities shatter your relationship.

CLEANSE FOR: trauma, freedom, balance and harmony, duality, break free from limitations

THE LEAP BETWEEN TIMELINES

He came to me worn down and weighted. He didn't even ask right away. He just sat, smiled, and listened to everything I said. Eventually, it spilled out. "Will I ever be loved?" Not tolerated. Not partnered. Loved.

Spirit came in softly; I floated away and saw into his life. Spirit showed me his relationship. The romance never really there. Spirit showed me his kids, his pride and joy. I could also see that somewhere along the way, he had forgotten what joy felt like. I could see his dreams at night. He dreamed of a love he had only ever seen through glass: on screens, in coachings, in carefully edited photos of other people's social media. He wanted to know if that kind of love could ever belong to him. Spirit didn't answer with a yes or no. Instead, I whispered,

"Keep going. Try again. Try differently." He sighed. "I've tried everything. I'm tired. "That's when Spirit opened the curtain for me and let me see into his shadows, his reflections. I saw it, clear as day. A parallel life. His life, if only he dared to claim it. He was older, but lighter. His shoulders no longer carried invisible weight. His kids were grown. He had love. Real love. She was younger. Beautiful. Wearing an orange bathing suit. Not because of the color, but because she chose it, just like she chose him.

They laughed. They touched like they meant it. It was alive. I shared what I saw. Gently. Not as a guarantee, but as a compass. A truth that could be if he allowed it. He smiled, but it did not reach all the way. Not yet. After he left, Spirit whispered, "Humans get scared when they see what's possible."

Because to leap into the possible means leaving behind the familiar even if the familiar is slowly erasing you.

Spirit told me he would likely go back to the same routine, the same mold, the same relationship where he folds himself small to fit. But maybe, just maybe, he'll remember the orange bathing suit.

And maybe one day, that thought will be louder than his fear.

BLACK AND WHITE CAT

- Remember balance is crucial to living a full and healthy life.
-A time of healing if you've been battling some sort of illness, injury, or emotional problem.
->Happy safe and pain free-
-Make your health a priority.
->JOB = move to a new home / city
->End a toxic relationship
-You are watched over by guardian angels / passed loved ones
-Work on better communication.
- Remember you have the power and magic to create everything you want in your life trust that you have the skills.
 -don't wait -the time to focus on your dreams is now
*Meditation and journaling, moon baths –
recommended
-Tibet, India

CLEANSE FOR: ying yang, find balance

THE CITY SHE FEARED

I had an online session with a woman, her face looked like it had not rested in years. The kind of face that still smiled politely, but the eyes gave it all away. The first thing she said to me was, "I don't know what's wrong with me anymore. Everything hurts, but I am not even sure if it is physical." My first feather showed me that she was desperately out of balance. Her body had been screaming for rest, but she ignored it. Her soul had been begging her to leave a toxic relationship, but she justified it. Her intuition had whispered about a move, a fresh start, but she drowned it in doubt and routines. Then her grandmother came through so clearly. A strong soul. She cried when I delivered her message. Not because it was news, but because deep down, she already knew. She had been blessed with her grandmother's and mother's strong will. But like many women, she gave every ounce of her energy away until there was nothing left for her.

Her body had started to ache in places the doctors could not diagnose. Her energy dropped even when she wasn't working. Her joy? Forgotten.

We did a deep cleanse, calling in balance, forgiveness, health.

Before she left, she said, "I've been thinking about moving somewhere new... I feel like there's something waiting for me there."

"There is," I said. "But it's not a place. It's you. The version of you that's already free and healed."

STINGRAY

-Know that everything is now in place.

-Know and be secure that you have the tools, the skills, and the ability to have everything you have worked towards open for you – so stop hesitating.

-Have faith in your abilities and follow your inner wisdom.

-Don't allow distractions or drama to sway you from your journey.

    *Complicated emotional issue

-Have you felt confined trapped, or off track?

->Redirect yourself to a healthier situation, seek out peace and patience

-Work with water

-Protect your boundaries.

-You are well on your way to achieving your goals -take action.

→ love

→ anger

→Give it 2-4 months

THE SOUND SHE NEEDED

She booked an online session. But the minute she logged in, I could feel her energy was heavy, like her body had been carrying something for too long. Then, I felt the pause of her heart, like it had gone missing in the noise of her life.

Her sadness wasn't loud it was quiet, stuck in her chest like a stone she didn't know how to move. She wasn't crying. She wasn't speaking much. But Spirit told me to speak softly, to hold space in a way she hadn't been held in a long time. So, I did.

I started describing what I saw: the way her emotions had been swirling, the tension in her body, the way her thoughts looped in cycles that drained her. She kept nodding, her eyes wide, like she was surprised someone else could feel the storm shed been fighting off with a broken umbrella. But I knew it because I too owned a broken umbrella once.

She didn't need deep prophecy. She needed direction. She needed someone to remind her that her life was not over. That she wasn't stuck forever. That just because she had been carrying anger, disappointment, and quiet grief didn't mean she had failed.

Spirit showed me that everything she needed was already in place. Her next step wasn't about doing more, it was about trusting herself again. Trusting that she had the ability to step back into her power, to protect her energy, and to stop letting the chaos around her decide how she felt inside.

By the end of the session, her body had softened. Her voice had steadied. She said, "You don't even know. Just hearing your voice made me feel like I could breathe again."

Sometimes people don't come for answers. Sometimes, they come to be reminded that they still exist.

WHITE CRAINE

-You are being guided through a phase-being aware of not having control can make anyone afraid. Know that Spirit is guiding you and protecting you.

-Don't feel alone, you have good people that surround you, lean on them.

-Don't exclude the unconventional approach-listen to your instincts.

->Home - sacred and protected

-> Be mindful of your relationship and responsibilities.

-Breathe - turn to every relaxation technique you know - Restore calmness

-Patience there are many situations in your life you can't force.

- Ground yourself regularly - you will discover more insights more quickly.

-Find unconventional ways to be self-reliant and productive no matter what, you can do it!

SHE WASN'T BROKEN, JUST TIRED

I listened to my client describe her life. She had been separated from her husband for five years. I asked her, why she came to see me. She said that she didn't come to me seeking answers or to be cleansed or unblocked. She just felt a need after watching Ivana's YouTube videos.

As she spoke, Holy Spirit told me that she came because she needed comfort, a space where she didn't have to explain or perform, just be.

I reached over and caressed her; I felt her emptiness. Her energy felt like someone who had been holding her

breath for a long time. Not in panic, but in quiet survival.
I knew it so well.

She had learned how to live on her own, how to manage, how to smile when she had to. But when I touched her chest and connected to her heart, I could feel that she was running on reserve, emotionally flatlined, not because she had nothing left to give, but because she hadn't allowed herself to receive.

Spirit didn't send me fire or a storm. It was soft. Calm. It asked me to slow her down. I held her. She had been so strong for so long, it almost felt unnatural for her to be held.

I led her through a meditation that wasn't about healing some grand trauma, it was about bringing her nervous system back home. Back to safety. Back to the sacred space she had forgotten she carried within her.

Not every session is fireworks. Sometimes, it's just an exhale. And that is just as holy.

IGUANA

-Nature can inspire you and bring you the healing you desire.

-Be satisfied and grateful for everything you have.

-You should shed everything in your life that isn't bringing you closer to your goals.

-Work on your psychic abilities -your intuition muscle

-Remember worrying isn't going to help you solve any of your problems.

-Be joyful in all situations and remain optimistic about things.

-Make time to be alone in meditation.

-Remember when the spotlight feels to be too much, it is ok to retreat and collet yourself.

-You are in a moment of stillness and observation, begin discerning those things of which you are not normally aware of.

-What makes you happy? What little things can you do daily to release your joy?

- With the period of personal growth, you've been going through you have shed old ways - become new- otherwise you would remain bound to the past in unhealthy ways.

- Remember we all have battles some simply can't be won. Know when you should step down and wait until the chaos passes before you jump back in the moment.

-Know that you have a powerful soul-there is little that truly frightens it.

-Know that you have a knack for showing people how the find fulfillment.

-Go at your own pace.

-Beware of emotional coldness when upset - let things go.
-Establish healthy boundaries.
-Seek guidance from ancient wisdom silent languages(signals)

PRAY FOR: manifesting contentment, more patience, stress levels, adaptability / change regeneration / healing

SHE SAW COLOR, BUT DIDN'T KNOW WHY

She was in the beauty industry, surrounded by faces, skin tones, lights, mirrors, and movement. But something had started quietly shifting inside her. She came to me through an online session. As her spirit animal message flowed out of me, I felt that she was unsure how to explain what was happening to her. Spirit then showed me that she came because she needed a mirror that reflected back her soul, not her face.

Then she interrupted, "I see colors around people now," she said softly, like it was a secret she wasn't sure she was allowed to speak aloud. But I already knew. What stood out to me wasn't just her gift, it was the timing. She was still wearing the old clothes of who she had to be in her career: polished, sharp, quick.

But her soul had started whispering a new language, and she was listening. Her body didn't quite understand it yet, but her spirit had already said yes. This session wasn't about decoding everything for her. It was about gently guiding her to trust what she already knew. I reminded her that not all gifts arrive with trumpets and light. Some arrive in silence, in stillness, in observation. I told her to keep watching. Keep breathing. Keep honoring the moments when her heart gets louder than her thoughts.

She smiled, relieved. It's like she had been walking barefoot on a path she didn't know existed, and I just pointed to her own feet and said, yes, you're exactly where you're supposed to be.

ROLY POLY

-New beginnings, change, and growth

-You need to release something negative from your life.

-Go play, reclaim your inner child, live in the moment.

- Remember we all must work but play is also a must for rejuvenation, self-love, and emotional health.

-Balance

-Protect yourself from those who don't have your best interest in mind.

-Set clear and protective boundaries.

-Embrace who you are and stand in your power.

*Practice water cleansings = baths / cold plunge

- Be open to change and willing to try new things.

- Be careful not to take things for granted, this will make you feel like you're stuck in a rut.

- Remember you're a survivor no matter what life throws at you; you find a way to overcome it.

→ Altar – set up safe and nurturing space for yourself.

CLEANSE FOR: renewal, regeneration, fertility / prosperity, protection, resilience, abundance, luck with love and relationships

ROLLING TOWARDS THE WHY

She was young, curious, and searching. Not in a desperate way, but in that restless way people get when they've already tried everything else. She told me she'd traveled the world collecting pieces of forbidden knowledge. A little bit of Indian spiritualism here, a touch of old European cards there.Psychics, palm readers, dream interpreters. She was drawn to all of it.

She was not broken, just trying so hard to get answers about her future that she forgot to live the moment she was in. When she sat down with me, I felt it right away. Spirit was clear: this was not about revealing timelines or soulmates. This was about helping her understand why she was chasing answers in the first place.

She had already been through therapy, yoga, meditation, and asked questions. But sometimes, even after doing everything right, the future stays silent. And that's not punishment, it is protection.

I did not dress it up and make her believe there was a secret I could unlock. I simply told her the truth: If Spirit does not hand it to me, it's not time. And if you are only here for predictions, you'll miss the healing that's being offered right now.

So instead, I guided her inward. We focused on her energy. I told her to go play again, to reconnect with the part of herself that she did not need to know everything she only needed to feel safe. In the end, I know she was a little disappointed, but I knew something had shifted. She wasn't dazzled. But something clicked. And sometimes that's enough.

STINK BUG

- Protection, grounding, introspection
-Look inward and evaluate your actions and choices - make sure they are aligned with your values and beliefs.
-Embrace personal growth and transformation, time to shed old ways.
-Beware - make well-informed decisions (don't assume).
*Practice mindfulness and meditation.
-Don't forget yourself.
-Be discreet and strategic with your actions don't share so much with the outside world (plans or business)
→conflict – avoid hostility (problematic individuals / blamers)
→shift in personality / traits = tend to resort to:

> → anger / fear / manipulation
> → smile but keep things in

-Remember there is more than one way to resolve a problem
PRAY FOR: Protection, awareness, patience, intuition

BLOCKS AND CLEANSE
Throat Chakra
WEAR: blue clothes and crystals
DRINK: peppermint tea
DO: neck stretches, yoga, journal

What spirit animal told me my client was suffering from: throat problems, tension and pain in the neck, shoulders and jaw, thyroid and lymph problems, teeth, gums, nose and ears, sinus, upper raspatory

SOME BATTLES AREN'T YOURS TO FIGHT

He came to me looking worn, exhausted but polite, like someone who had held too many things in for too long. I could already feel the weight in his shoulders, the tension in his jaw. All of this was causing him to lose his hair. He didn't need to tell me where it hurt. Spirit showed me: throat, neck, jaw, pressure behind the eyes. That kind of pain is not just physical, it is emotional.

As I delivered his spirit animal message, his father came through: "Tell him it's okay to let go." Not of the situation, but of the need to fix it all. The brother. The sister. The drama. The blame. It was not his job to hold the family together with silence and migraines.

There is a specific kind of suffering that comes from people pleasing in chaotic families. You become the peacekeeper, the listener, the quiet one with all the headaches. And over time, your body starts to speak for you.

His father shared love for all of the family but with that came a message for him, his son, to stop. To stop sharing so much with people who twist his words. To stop apologizing for stepping away from conflict he never asked to be part of. He needed boundaries, not bravery. His father's spirit helped me deliver words from spirit animal, wear your blue, stretch your neck, sip peppermint tea like it is medicine. Write your rage down. We did a cleanse on his Chakra throat and reminded him not to mute his voice, use it with power, not panic. I hope he became the big brother his inner child waited for.

SEAL

-Be aware of your thoughts and dreams, it is time to pay close attention to your thoughts and insight.

-It is time to allow your imagination to soar, follow your dreams.

-Listen to your inner self:

>visions- feed creative imagination

->Follow your body's natural rhythms.

-Embrace your inner child, let go of your fears of the unknown. Find happiness in your life through humor.

-Energetic agility

- Be an active listener, sometimes your emotions shape your perception in such a way that you may not hear what someone is meaning when they speak.

>Master your emotions = place a protective layer of emotional protection from hasty or aggressive people.

> Move away from the need for every advice and find quiet time for you.

-Keep going, don't let anything stop you.

-Keep joy in your heart

CLEANSE FOR: grounding, anxiety, stress, peace, strength, optimism, aggressiveness, clumsy, sensitivity

THE DREAM SHE ALMOST GAVE UP ON

She walked in heavy not with anger, but with the kind of grief that floats just below the skin. You could feel it before she even said a word. Her energy was timid, like someone who once believed in magic but got robbed of it somewhere along the way.

Her grandfather came through clear, thick southern accent, warm and protective. He stood beside her like a wall. He didn't waste time with formalities. "Tell her it's not her fault," he said. "Tell her the dream still matters."

Spirit doesn't always explain things gently. He spoke about the friend, how he'd taken advantage of her, how he had stolen more than money. He had taken the one thing that kept her going: the hope. The plans. The sneaker shop dream that lived inside her chest like a heartbeat.

We didn't talk about revenge. We didn't talk about forgiveness. We cleansed what had gotten stuck, the fear that it would happen again. The distrust in her own ability to tell good from bad. That trembling panic that comes when you don't feel safe around your own ideas anymore.

She did not need to be told to dream again. Her grandfather had already done that.

He reminded her that her emotions are not weaknesses. That her sensitivity is a gift. That she must protect it, not numb it.

That it is okay to retreat sometimes. To laugh again. To trust her rhythm. To open the notebook and sketch the menu of that little café even if the world isn't ready yet.

She left still a little shaken. But lighter. Like someone who might just buy the domain name for her business again when she got home.

BLUE MOON BUTTERFLY

-End of a phase / metamorphosis
-Have you stopped dancing?
-Do you need help transitioning from one stage of life to the next?
-Connect to the wisdom of your ancestors.
-It is ok to ease your way through change creatively while celebrating your life.
-But know that it is time for personal growth and greater awareness of your mental, physical, and spiritual rhythms.
7 - 8 days
        Madagascar, Asia, Australia
*You cannot embrace the new you until you fully release the old you!
- Observe elements of your character, morals, and habits that weigh you down -> they no longer belong to you and are keeping you stuck in a mire of negative energy.
-> The goal is to embrace changes in your emotional body.
- Remember you are on a long soul journey.
 •Everything in life is temporary.
-Explore your creativity and intuition.
-Break free from limitations.

PRAY FOR: Calm decision making, self-expression, better communication and speech

BLOCK AND CLEANSE
Throat Chakra
DO: medical blue light therapy

DRINK: herbal tea, cacao, water
EAT: Blue berries, kelp, dragon fruit, raw honey

What spirit animal told me my client was suffering from: shoulder tension, teeth grinding, jaw, underactive thyroid

THE GENTLE FLIGHT BACK TO LIFE
When he came to see me, I could smell it, the thick, stale scent of shock and abandonment. That's part of my psychic ability, smelling situations, things, feelings. I am also able to sense and smell where the pain lives in the body before it is spoken. I could smell so many answers before he walked in the room. He was frail. Timid. Sweet in that way some people are when life has stripped them bare but left a little softness behind. His wife had left him. Gone far away to the islands. Left him standing in the ruins of a life they built together, confused about how quickly love can pack its bags and vanish.
He did not say much, but his spirit's smell spoke volumes. And then, his childhood friend came through. Spirit has a way of sending the right ones. This friend, this soul from school days, had a gentle way of reminding him who he was before the heartbreak. They joked, they reminisced, but more than that he helped me deliver the message of the Blue Moon Butterfly.
"You are not dead," the friend said. "You're just between versions of yourself." So, we did a cleanse, for his shoulder tension, for the grind in his jaw, for the words caught in his throat where love used to live. He slipped into hypnosis while I untangled the grief sitting

in his lymph and thyroid. I told him it's okay to ease into change. To stop asking who he was with her and start asking who he is now. To take one small trip, even just to the next town. To explore a new place. To buy the ticket. To live again. I prayed with him. Not the kind of prayer that begs, just the kind that remembers his soul came here for more than suffering.

And I like to believe, wherever he is now, he's somewhere warm, with a passport, a journal, and a smile no longer stolen by the past.

FROG

*Luck

*You are being reminded to address your feelings and emotions rather than ignoring them. -Feelings allow you to grow.

-(Severe life changes – awakenings and transformations)

*Abundance on all levels

-Enhance your intuition and strengthen your connection to the spirit world. You are coming into your power, make your choices based on what is right for you.

→Stay close to home where your "family" is – it is essential to be close to parents (elders)

→ Release emotions (anger, sadness, bitterness, hatred) = Dark spots on aura = leaving you vulnerable!

-Relationship - no return

! SELF LOVE!

-Remember you have natural intuitive senses and require strong spiritual connections to maintain your power and vision.

DETOX- throat Chakra -take care with diet and exercise, moon cleansings, intentional shower baths, sound baths

PRAY FOR: fertility, prosperity, rebirth, and growth

BLOCKS AND CLEANSE:
Throat Chakra
WEAR: Turquoise color, blue crystals
DO: burn blue candles
CHANT: SO HUM
GO: Italy

JOB: Advice giver / counselor

What spirit animal told me my client was suffering from: Block from growth. An unhealed wound and inability to celebrate life in all of its incarnations. Problems with endocrine gland/thyroid.

THE SACRED RETURN

She came to me through a screen. Thousands of miles away, and yet I felt her like thunder in my chest. Her voice was small, but the energy around her was enormous, swollen with silence, burdened with memory. As a young child, she had been locked in a cabinet. They left her alone in the dark in extreme fear. Mental illness and the voices in her head became her identity. As she got older, something inside her never truly came out from the darkness.

During our session, the Holy Spirit lifted the veil between her pain and mine. I felt it. The bone-deep fear that doesn't have words. The one I knew too well from my own childhood story.

I whispered chants that carried old prayers. Then miles apart, I guided her on a soul retrieval. We spoke to the little girl who was never meant to be forgotten. We gave her a place inside her grown-up self.

We called back her pieces, one by one from the corners of time where they had been buried, still locked away in the dark, unloved.

She had blocked so much of her growth because she had never given herself permission to feel, let alone celebrate. So, we opened that space together, with gentle breathwork, sacred affirmations, and a whispered promise that her story did not end in the dark.

It ends in color.

And when I look in the mirror now and again, I still think of her. I pray fiercely that she has found what we all long for: a moment of peace inside herself. Trust in people. Faith in something greater. And a deep, defiant love for the woman she is now.

Because sometimes, the most sacred return is the one back to yourself.

GECKKO
*Luck, renewal, regeneration
-Your goals are never out of reach.
*Be highly adaptable, accept change when it comes and accept adversity as an opportunity to improve yourself.
*Be more attentive to your dreams.
->Give fear no place in your life you can triumph over anything.
->Know what you want in your life and go after it, do not let anyone discourage you.
-Stop wasting your time and energy on things that don't improve your life.
* Spiritually gifted > planes of consciousness
-Healing = you or your loved one will soon recover.
*Financial need
-Be honest in serious situations, where feelings are on the line!
-Self care = lose the guilt

FAMILY JEWELS
It started like it often does, with curiosity, slow and uncertain. She said she didn't know what to expect, that she had never done anything like this before. But her eyes told me something else. They had the look of someone who had been waiting for answers longer than she wanted to admit. She didn't sit like someone lost. She sat like someone tired. Like someone who had held everything together so well for so long, no one noticed she was still hurting. I knew immediately we were not dealing with just one question. We were standing in the

middle of a hallway full of unopened doors. Before I could say anything, her mother came through. She was gentle, but immediate, like someone stepping into a warm kitchen from a storm.

There was no awkward introduction, no delay, just the unmistakable sense of familiarity, like they had been waiting to speak again since the day they last did. Then the father arrived. His energy was slower, more thoughtful, like a man who did not rush when he spoke in life either. He showed me papers having to do with a house. A new home. A place she knew she needed to move toward, but kept doubting, because she didn't know if it was her time. Because she was scared of starting over again. Because the dream was hers, and no one else's. But it wasn't just about the move. It was about her brother, too. Her parents gave her warnings, not out of fear, but out of truth. A gentle redirection. A reminder that her role as the "fixer" had reached its expiration. That love does not always mean carrying someone else's chaos in your own chest. Her parents spoke of the lost jewelry and where she would find it. They discussed her business. The dogs. The land. The tangled web of passion and burnout she couldn't tame. Spirit then reminded her that her compassion is holy, but not infinite. That it needs direction. That her gifts were meant to lift not exhaust her. She promised to look again in the dresser, for the jewels. To take the next step. To say no to what no longer healed her. Her reading reminded me how when the family aligns both here and beyond it's like the whole universe adjusts its light to help you find your way back to yourself.

MONKEY

*Prepare for the unexpected.

-Remember that playfulness and entertainment are useful for the soul.

-Remember your journey on this planet is not a solitary one.

- Use your ingenuity and resourcefulness to solve problems. Remain honest with yourself.

-Humor = motivator – use laughter to heal

-Find play time

-Remember that your time on earth touches many other people. Reach out to your group and hold them dear.

-Relationships - How you speak and listen and look at the situation really matters!

*Consider your best course of action by reflecting on all the consequences.

*Maintain bonds you've established with family and friends

-Move / travel

*Commitment to your group - Do the members, integrity, ethics, and ways align with me?

A SCENTED PERFUME

Her body carried a quiet inflammation. Her shoulders pressed up toward her ears. Her chest barely moved when she breathed, as if even her lungs were unsure if they were allowed to expand. Her perfume smelled like guilt. Guilt does not always shout; sometimes it hums under the skin like an allergic reaction you've grown used to.

Holy Spirit showed me her mind. There was a secret she had wrapped around her body like a second skin. Her family had lived a whole life under one truth. Her daughter, already grown now, a woman of her own was not her husband's child. Not biologically. But raised in his love. Raised in the shared silence. Even the son, who had called her sister since childhood, never knew. It wasn't meant to be cruel. She wasn't a liar by nature. But life, when you're young and afraid, doesn't always offer you soft places to land. She made a choice. Then time passed. And passed. And kept on passing until she could not remember where the beginning of the story even was. Spirit showed me what was coming. A baby, her daughter's baby. Medical tests. A trail of questions that would lead right back to the truth she had been hiding. The secret was going to come out whether she was ready or not. But Spirit, in all its mercy, was not cruel about it. It did not threaten her with consequences. It offered her a choice. Tell the truth now, or let it unravel later without her guidance. And I knew, in my heart, that this was not just about her family knowing. This was about her body. Her swelling. Her exhaustion. Her deep, aching nervous system that was tired of holding this story all by itself. But she didn't want to hear it. Not at first. Not even after I described the entire story, from beginning to end. She argued with me. She said it would ruin everything. She said it would be easier to let it come out later, if it had to. But Spirit showed me the truth in her bloodstream, in the quiet tremble of her hands, she was already unraveling, quietly, from the inside. And no healing could reach her until that weight was released.

Secrets like that, they fester. They settle in your thyroid, your skin, your breath, your joints. They weigh down your light. I don't know if she did it. I truly hope she did. Not for her daughter. Not for her husband. Not for the story. But for herself.

SEA CUCUMBER

-Healing and protection, regeneration of your body
*Emotion and intuition
-Heal the world with your compassion and kindness.
-Take time for yourself.
*Remember you are all in it together, your actions have ripple effects that touch everyone on his planet.
↳ Let go of what no longer serves you.
-Have hope, faith, and perseverance. Remember you have the power and strength to overcome.
*Water baths
*Chinese medicine
-Now is a good time to take inventory of your life and make changes for the better.

PRAY FOR: rebirth / renewal, pregnancy

BLOCKS AND CLEANSE:
Sacral Chakra
EAT: orange foods
DRINK: Yin Yun, citrus, cinnamon, jasmine teas
DO: Goddess pose
GET: a new hobby

What spirit animal told me my client was suffering from: Menstrual cramps, UTI, back pain, closed off, uncomfortable with own body, shame

THE QUIET RETURN

She arrived wrapped in tension. Her smile was polite, but her eyes reflected a lifetime of waiting. She didn't ask for a psychic reading. She didn't want to talk to the dead. She just asked for a cleanse, softly, like someone testing the waters, afraid even her voice might break the possibility of something new.

She had spent years chasing motherhood like it was running away from her. She didn't use those words, but her body told the story, frustrated, stiff, holding guilt in places where life was supposed to grow. Late forties, years of loss, and a silence around her pain so loud it followed her into every room. She told me she just wanted a baby. That is all. Just a baby.

I didn't ask why she waited. I didn't ask how many doctors she had seen. I didn't ask why her voice shook when she said "IVF." I just started the cleanse. Gently. Thoroughly. With herbs to call her back into her own body.

She closed her eyes and let herself feel again, maybe for the first time in years. The meditation was soft. No visions, no messages from beyond. Just breath and warmth and the hum of something opening. After the silence settled, Spirit gave me one clear message: She will get pregnant. But not naturally. Through medicine. When I told her, she blinked slowly, almost unsure if she had heard me right. She sat very still and then whispered, "Thank you."

We didn't talk about miracles. We didn't talk about time. We talked about trust. Trusting her own body. Trusting the decision to get help. Trusting herself to stop hiding her hope from everyone, including herself.

WESTERN SPOTTED ORB WEAVER

* Creativity *

-Creation of life-

- Remember that you are the engineer of your destiny, now is the time to catch your dreams and take advantage of all the things that present themselves.

* There are no obstacles in your path, go for it!

-We have seen your patience, perseverance, and hard work. Stay focused on your work.

-Do not give up on setbacks and obstacles.

*Work - karma

-Remember the interconnectedness between us and the world around

-Create, create, create

Remember despite every obstacle you face; you should never get discouraged or lose faith in yourself.

HER MOVE

She came in with that look I've seen too many times. Like the city had chewed her up and spit her back out. Blank stare. Soul limping. The kind of defeated that doesn't make a sound. Not tears or rage. Just a silence so heavy it pulls the shoulders down. She had been spun around, knocked over, and sent back to the village to remember how to breathe again.

She didn't need to say a word. Her energy walked in before she did. Worn like a coat that had been soaked through in a storm and never dried. After prayer, I closed my eyes and saw into her. The pressure. The invisible wounds. The endless proving. Her body was thin, pale, fragile, but her spirit? Her spirit was massive. Spirit made sure I saw it glow.

Then someone came through for her. A man with academic energy. The kind of presence that holds both structure and softness. He came in sharp, dressed neat, holding books, pointing to papers being written late into the night. He showed me a classroom. Her ambition. Her fire before it got buried. He was proud of her. He needed her to remember.

Then I saw that she had been back home, living with her family after studying abroad, healing, yes, but also hiding. The city had done a number on her, and she was not sure she had it in her to keep going.

She said it was her professor. He said, "She doesn't need more healing before she starts. She's ready now." Then she said, almost in a whisper, "I want to work at the UN. I always have."

Holy Spirit came with instructions and specific guidance on what documents needed refreshing, what steps to take. It was precise. Sharp. Loving, but not coddling.

I watched her spirit stand back up. I didn't need to explain her body remembered. Her field brightened. The fire returned to her eyes. It wasn't about feeling better. It was about remembering who she was before the world tried to make her forget. Spirit didn't show up with soft comfort.

That session wasn't a miracle. It was a remembering. Spirit had seen all the healing she'd already done. Now it was time for her to make her move.

BLACK CAT

*Psychic

-Do not let any social stigmas take that away from you.

*Feeling shunned and left out.

-Grow and remain flexible.

*Do not succumb to the idea that somehow you are bad luck to those around you or are somehow lesser than them. When this happens, reach out and get love from those you love. You deserve it.

*Rumors, trying to make you feel unworthy or oppressing you in any way.

*Abandonment Issues

-Stand up for prejudice.

JOB / CALLING: Support and advocacy – adoption

CLEANSE FOR: authority, elegance, adaptability, focus, independence, intuition/ tapping into the supernatural and sensual self

SHE WAS NEVER THE CURSE

She came in quiet but tense, holding her breath. I could feel her every emotion in my own body. My hands were sweaty, and my stomach turned. I felt like vomiting. After prayer, I felt her mother come through like a force. Like when your mom comes in to yell at you for picking on your little brother. Strong. Protective. No hesitation. Her presence came through immediately and took over the space.

She did not waste a single second. She showed me into her world, the fights with her brother and his wife after their mom died. Then her mother laid it out clearly: the way the family had been treating her, the way they were trying to dim her, quiet her, contain her into something she never was. She showed me the way her daughter had been carrying the weight of guilt that wasn't hers, being made to feel like the black sheep, the difficult one, the problem. But Spirit was not having that narrative anymore. Her mother told her it was time to step back, not to disconnect out of anger, but to give time and space for truth and healing to grow between them all. She needed to get out of that house. Out of that town. Out of their energy. She needed to remember who she was without all those old eyes watching her every move with judgment and assumptions.

She needed to live. To travel. To explore. To fall in love. To find someone who chose her the way she deserved to be chosen. And her mother didn't say maybe, she said it would happen. She said her daughter would have her own family, her own home, far away, and that she would walk with her the entire time. No matter where she went, she wouldn't be alone.

I could feel how much she needed to hear it. Not the prediction, the permission. The validation that she wasn't broken. That she wasn't unlucky or too much or hard to love. That she was never the one bringing pain into the room. That was projection and fear. That wasn't hers to carry.

I hope she listened. I hope she allowed her own intuition to lead. I hope she found her way to places where her difference wasn't feared but celebrated.

AZURE BLUE JAY

-You are being reminded that to wear the crown of true mastership requires dedication, responsibility, and committed development in all things physical as well as spiritual.

- Granted access to memories long forgotten > assimilate them into awareness

-Remember that risk taking, seizing new opportunities, and discovering new adventures are what life is all about.

↳Use the power of your intelligence and courage. Balance these with discreet silence and the utmost patience and timing.

*Be bold and curious.

→Embrace learning, new ideas and concepts.

-Remember mental growth aids spiritual growth.

Family

$ Management / banking

->Scandalous gossip = avoid

*Beware of setting plans in motion only to abandon them. Make firm choices and follow through.

*Inner child

-Practice gentleness

PRAY FOR: Renewal, transformation, growth, communication

BLOCKS AND CLEANSE

Throat Chakra

DO: Neck exercises, breathwork, journal, manifest on paper

EAT: Blue berries, carrots, goji berries, plums

Third Eye Chakra
DO: Guided meditation, visualization, work with your own memories, color, draw, sun gaze, practice yoga

TRUTH IN TWO FREQUENCIES

They came in together. She sat closest to me. She was the one speaking. He was just there. Silent, respectful, drained. She was only here to offer him support because she wanted me to "heal him." I already knew the session was not going to be what she thought it would be. Spirit does not cater to control.

I did not answer. I just listened. Spirit started speaking before I even opened my mouth.

The Azure Blue Jay came forward, not just as a symbol, but as a divider of truth. One bird. Two wings. Two very different energies. The Blue Jay pointed, this part is for him, this part is for her.

And so, after delivering the spirit animal message, I guided them both to meditation. The sound of my voice instantly hypnotized him and soothed him. He did not need to be told anything; he needed to feel something, peace, permission, release. So, I used my voice, slowly and gently. The moment he closed his eyes; he slipped deep into rest. Not escape. Not avoidance. Restoration. Spirit took him into a state of pure stillness, while I stayed with her.

Her body was tight. Her face tried to hold form, but the vibration in the room cracked through it. She was not cruel, she was lost. She had not been nurturing her life, only managing his. Spirit made it clear: this journey was not about healing him, it was about returning her to herself. So I guided her, not with ideas, but with vibration.

We continued on with the meditation as his loud snores filled the stillness in the room. I walked her back to her inner child. The one she'd hidden under routines, sacrifices, and anxiety. I didn't tell her what to do. I just stood with her while she saw who she had become, and who she still was beneath all that weight.

When it was done, he opened his eyes smiling like a man who had touched joy. His first words were, "Thank you." He kissed both my hands with reverence. It wasn't about me, it was the energy he had returned to. Something soft. Something real. Something his.

She didn't speak. She stayed quiet, still guarded, still deciding. Not everyone walks out of a session transformed. But something inside her shifted. I know it did. Spirit never brings people together without a reason. I don't know what happened to them. Maybe they separated. Maybe they grew. Maybe they stayed stuck in the pattern. That's not my work. My work is to remind people of who they are when they forget. Spirit does the rest.

CRAB

-It is time to change course and go in a new direction.
?*Are you having a difficult time going with the flow?
?*Is emotional vulnerability difficult for you?
?*Do you want to go in a new direction but feel stuck?
*Know that you are protected from vulnerable discoveries and personal weaknesses when they are not ready to open up.
-Know that you will always embody happy domesticity.
! Avoid situations for something safer - meaning, navigate or avoid this in a less direct manner
-Know that you are very strong and resistant, do not give up those things which you have earned rightfully.
->Prepare for a period of renewal and rebirth but know that you may feel defenseless during this process of change. Until that new environment manifests, proceed with caution.
*Partner – drive – be gentle
-Talisman
- Don't be afraid, but in order to tap into your creativity or to fund inspiration, you must explore your inner thoughts, emotions and imagination deeply.
! One message - change your path
*Take time away from all the noise and unsolicited advice, meditate and listen to your own heart.
? What is it that has always captured your mental or spiritual curiosity?
-Confront what holds you back even if its uncomfortable – procrastination, low self-esteem, resistant to change.
*Don't hide in your shell.

*It is time to let your light shine.
→ You are safely guided to the next great opportunity in your journey.
→ Strengthen your auric field with cold water / moon water. (Negative emotions, guilt vibration)
→You have the heart of a lion.
→ Move in your own unique way.

<u>BLOCKS AND CLEANSE</u>
Root Chakra
EAT: Red diet, potatoes, carrots, parsnips, onions, garlic
-BURN: Frankincense and cedar wood oil
-LISTEN- 396 Hz frequency
-SAY: I AM affirmations for security

What spirit animal told me my client was suffering from: Panic, worry, overthinking, depression, bad dreams, anger, sex dysfunction, somatization, out of balance, rushing, exhausted, lethargic, uninspired, stuck, inability to take action, powerless or lack of control

THE DUAL CURRENTS
She booked the session, but he came too. I don't usually allow that. Spirit has to give the nod because this is sacred space, and not everyone deserves access to someone else's unraveling. But Spirit was quiet. Not welcoming, not rejecting. Just watching. So, I let it slide. The moment I began the reading; I felt the split. It happened fast. First plane, his father. Already there, already waiting. He did not hesitate. He just started talking. Told me everything about his son, my uninvited guest. About the ache he carried, the things he never said, the walls

he built, and the boy still curled behind them. Spirit let me into that space and held it open just wide enough. I didn't speak to him directly. I didn't have to. The father came through and guided my hands to do a cleanse, quiet, energetic, unannounced. A soft, untraceable recalibration. One man holding space for another from the other side. But I didn't say a word or even looked in his direction. All this happened telepathically, he remained unaware of everything, I knew. But his soul knew, his soul still knows what happened in that room.

Second plane her. Present, eager, heavy with expectation. She wanted to know if this was it. If he was the one. If Spirit could give her permission to keep bending herself in his direction. But Spirit held me tighter than usual. I wasn't allowed to speak the things she came to hear. Instead, Spirit showed me her entire life in fragments, acts of service disguised as love, self-sacrifice passed off as commitment. She had never really been in her life. Only adjacent to it. Always in someone else's orbit, never at her own center. Spirit didn't let me spell it out. I read between the lines. Let the moments breathe. Let the clock tick loud enough to speak for me. She didn't need predictions. She needed pause because in my readings, silence has its own language. They left together. Still linked but not aligned. I knew they wouldn't last. Spirit had already shown me the endings. But some things aren't for me to say aloud. You don't rip the thread while someone's still sewing. I still see them, every now and then. Separately. She tries hard to rebuild. He tries hard to forget. They both work hard. But in different directions now.

MOURNING DOVE

- Period of peace, hope, and renewal
-Follow your heart, this is a situation where you are being asked to walk in faith and be true to yourself.
-Remember to soar you must know when to move your wings and allow the wind to take you to new heights.
-Surrender and allow the wind to support your wings, get moving so that you can feel the joy of flying higher and higher.
*Breath work -find peace
-Know that change and what you're looking for is just around the corner.
*Purify your thoughts-you are attracting what you don't want by focusing on it.
*End of problematic cycle in your life
*New romance. New beginnings. New friendships. Healing.

BLOCKS AND CLEANSE:
Crown Chakra
WEAR: Violet colors and clear quarts
TAKE: Melatonin
DO: Breathwork and fasting
EAT: Mushrooms, garlic, ginger, onion, lychee, coconut

Third eye Chakra
WEAR: Purple clothes, crystals
DRINK: Raw cacao, star anise tea
EAT: honey, coconut oil
DO: Prayer, meditation, visualization, sun gaze, breath work

What spirit animal told me my client was suffering from: Headache, clogged sinuses, memory loss, anxiety, dizziness, lack of focus

THE SECRET SHE KEPT

She booked an online session saying she needed clarity, but the moment I connected with her, I felt something much heavier. Her energy was delicate, almost like she was trying to hold herself together. Right away, a presence stepped in, it was an older man, stubborn in life but soft in Spirit.

I described him, and before she could say much, I told her, "Your father-in-law is here." His presence was strong, but not aggressive. He came with something to say and he wasn't wasting time. I felt his guilt, his apology, his awareness of how cruel or distant he had been to her while he was alive. And then, almost like a secret he was pulling from behind her heart, he said, "She knows about my son's affair." That's when I looked at her and said,

"He wants me to talk to you about his son's affair." She went still; her eyes got big. She nodded slowly. "Yes," she said. "But I never told anyone. I never even told him." She had buried it deep. Lived with it. Slept next to it. Carried it like a ghost inside her body. Her father-in-law continued, he wanted her to know that his son was not like him. That it had been one tragic mistake, not a reflection of who he was as a man.

And that she deserved to let it go. She had protected everyone's peace but her own. She did not need spiritual advice from me, she just needed someone to witness the pain she had never spoken aloud.

After her cleanse, I could feel the soft energy of peace, hope, and grace. She did not cry hard. She just let go. In her own way. In her own time. And for the first time in years, I think she finally felt seen.

CROW

*Don't be afraid to use your voice powerfully to speak with integrity.

-Change: everything you have been working towards is coming to fruition.

*Pay attention to your thoughts.

->Spreading yourself too thin

      ->Take a step back, release where you are, and take inventory of your dreams and desires.

-> We see your integrity and bless you.

• Remember time is linear – that is why you are one of the ones that feels past, present, and future.

*Don't over question your intelligence.

→Don't fear change.

BLOCKS AND CLEANSE:

Solar Plexus Chakra (12-18 yrs)

What spirit animal told me my client was suffering from: Digestion and adrenal glands, bloating, cramps, nausea, diabetes, shortness of breath, weight, tiered, distressed, hard time taking action

THE FEELING

He returned to me for a second reading, walking in with the same heavy energy he had carried the first time, still wrapped in confusion and frustration, still attached to the problematic relationship he had come asking about before. Nothing had changed, not externally, and more importantly, not within him. He sat in front of me, speaking with that same searching tone, hoping for answers, but Spirit showed me this wasn't about love anymore, not real love, not the kind that heals and expands. This time, Spirit showed me the truth of his actions. He had been unfaithful in his relationship, not once or twice, but often, and rather than confront the emotional wreckage he was creating, he had turned to food, to overconsumption, trying to soothe the growing hole inside of him.

The worst part wasn't the cheating, it was the fact that he had been shown what to do in his last reading, given clear, loving direction by Spirit, and he had chosen to turn away from it, not because it wasn't true, but because it required change, and he wasn't ready. But here's the part that stung in a different way, he didn't come back seeking clarity or accountability. He returned for the feeling.

For the space I hold. For the way my voice softens his internal noise and lets him feel, just for that hour, like he's connected to something greater. He came for the high of my energy, not the wisdom of Spirit. But, Spirit didn't allow me to pour into him like I normally do. Instead, I allowed him to speak, to release, to fill the room with his thoughts like a man in therapy. And while he spoke, Spirit gently took me by the hand and showed me the truth: this man was not a bad person, but he was closed, hardened, and deeply attached to his own patterns.

His heart had not yet cracked open. His devotion was not to love or healing, but to work, to productivity, control, and the comfort of his own mind. And that is where he belonged right now, not in the world of partnership, not in deep intimacy, and not in my field.

That reading wasn't for him. It was for me. It was a mirror, a chance for me to see the difference between a seeker and someone who simply craves the light of others to mask their own shadows. Spirit reminded me of the sacredness of my own energy, of how vital it is to guard it with reverence and not let it be siphoned by those who do not intend to rise with it.

And so, I held the line. I let him feel what he came to feel, but I did not pour. I did not open the channel in full. And when he left, I did not wonder if he would change, I already knew he would not. But I also knew that I had.

HAWK

*Bigger picture
*Time to look at your situation from a different perspective.
-It is time to free yourself from thoughts and beliefs that are limiting your ability to soar above your life.
-Get a glimpse of the bigger picture; this will allow you to survive and flourish.
*Move in harmony with others.
*Fear- keeping your feelings caged, hurt, and unable to fly
*mental blocks
        ->whole new level of awareness is developing in your mind
-Know that you are surrounded by angels, divas, and the Devine
* Focus on what's ahead- leadership role
-Time to begin working with new divination methods
→ We see you learning to trust your inner guidance and higher self.
-Do not brush off gut instincts.
*Observation – Make swift, decisive, and successful movements.
*It is time for you to pause and pay attention to everything.
->It is time for you to ask yourself about the company you keep.

CLEANSE FOR: Clear vision, signs, omens, angel messages, better life perspective on jobs and relationships

THE RELEASE OF TEARS

She came to see me carrying a heavy hope wanting to know if her mother would come through. That was all she asked for. She sat down with soft eyes and a quiet voice, but I could feel the weight before she even spoke. So, I closed my eyes, left this realm and went looking for her mom in my visions. I didn't see her. I called her with my voice and waited, but her mother didn't come through the way she had hoped.

I placed my hand out to reach for her answers, but still nothing came. Spirit showed me that my client was too much in grief, and her mom's vibration could not reach her there. Spirit told her to lift up, not to chase her mother's ghost, but to find healing in the act of feeling. I placed my hands gently on her shoulders and guided her to my treatment table.

Her body was already unraveling. She was trying to hold herself together, but the tears had already begun. Quiet at first, and then they grew into sobs, loud, raw, aching sobs that shook the room like a storm coming in from the mountains.

I guided her into meditation. Together, we created a space where her mother could meet her, not through the veil in the way clients often expect, but through the heart. Through breath. Through surrender. And the moment she closed her eyes, she met her.

She saw her. Not in words, not in explanations, but in presence. A familiar energy washed over her, and her crying deepened. I didn't interrupt. I simply sang a lullaby that held the space for her to let go of what she had carried for too long. For almost an hour, she cried with the kind of grief that does not ask for permission. The grief that the body has been storing in bones, in breath, in the corners of memory we lock away. And when it was done, when her breathing began to soften and her fingers finally relaxed, she opened her eyes, her cheeks soaked, and her chest hollowed out from release. She said she felt better.

And I told her what Spirit told me: that it was not the reading, it wasn't even the vision of her mother. It was her tears. Her own medicine. The healing came through allowing what she had denied herself for so long, to cry, to let it pour out, to grieve without restraint or apology. Sometimes Spirit holds back not to punish, but to prepare.

ARMY WORM

*Destructive behavior – despite these tendencies you are resilient / survivalist

-Change and transformation – seasons change / life cycle

-Overwhelming situation / problem prepare for sudden change

*Remember there is power in community.

-Remember your colors and know that some things appearing delectable are not always good for you.

! Haste makes waste.

-Treasure what nourishes you and let go of the past.

*Fine tune your intuition to sense the non-verbal and nonphysical things around you.

- It is time to embrace your spiritual inheritance as a child of the universe.

*Beware of people who lie and give you false hope. Don't rush into fast decisions, especially in business.

-Patience ->power in secrecy

-12 eyes

-Safeguard your creative domain.

 CLEANSE FOR: strength, order from chaos, fear, unchecked expansion, over consumption, unsustainable practices, rapid growth, humility and meekness, feelings of stuck in a rut

THE UNSEEN BATTLES AND QUIET SURVIVAL

He walked in with a stillness that wasn't calm. He was in his late thirties, maybe early forties. He didn't say much at first, just that he wanted to feel. Not know, not solve, just feel. That was the first truth he gave me, and

Spirit heard it loud and clear. Before I could even begin the reading, the room shifted. The air felt fuller. His father's presence entered softly, but firmly, with the kind of energy that doesn't ask for attention, it commands it through love. He helped me deliver the Army Worm's message, an unlikely spirit animal, but deeply appropriate.

Spirit doesn't send animals for their prettiness or their popularity, it sends what the soul needs. And this man needed truth. Survival. Resilience. A reminder that just because you have been destructive at times, doesn't mean you're not still worthy of a second life. Or a third. Or a fourth. His father began to speak. Not in riddles, not in whispers but in warmth. Direct and clear.

He spoke about his son's health, his body, his habits, the things he knows he needs to shift but keeps pushing off. He spoke of his son's heart and blood health. He gave him specific directions guided and laced with love so palpable it brought tears to my eyes. I cried not just for him, but for myself.

Because in that moment, I realized I had never known that kind of paternal tenderness. Spirit showed me he was stuck in a pattern of overconsumption of energy, of distraction, of false promises.

He had surrounded himself with people who liked his potential but didn't nurture his soul. He was giving too much away too fast, especially in business. Spirit warned: "Beware of sweet talkers.

Not everything that glitters is meant to be touched." I walked away from that reading feeling full like something ancient had been healed just by being witnessed. His father didn't just speak to his son that day. He spoke to me. He spoke to every part of me that longed for the love of a father.

ALLIGATOR

-All of the unbridled creative forces of the world including fury and ferocity are with you.

-Balance yourself.

-Intuition, strength, and determination

-New power, new knowledge waiting to be born

-Stillness is strength, show your power by waiting to act.

-Take a step back and reassess what you really want in life.

-Observe your surroundings and tap into your internal dialogue.

-When you know what to look for, waiting becomes easy.

-Soon it will be a good time to come up for air and go towards what you desire.

-When you set your mind on something nothing will get in your way.

-Remember, you can live in many different types of habitats.

-If you are feeling alone or isolated, it is time to socialize. Reach out to your friends and family.

-Pay close attention to your life balance.

-Are you getting rest? Are you supporting yourself with a strong foundation or are you trying to get it all done?

-The way you move matters, move with purpose, poise, and grace.

-Find what you are putting off in your life and attack it with intensity, go at it with full force.

-Stand your ground, you have the power to protect yourself and those you love.

-Go outside, close your eyes, listen to the sound around you for two minutes. Tap into your senses other than your eyesight.
-Live in the moment, don't worry about the past or future.
-Ask yourself questions in your journal:
-Are you really happy? Be honest. If not, answer your questions with honesty to help yourself grow.
-Things have been moving slowly but you are put on notice that it is time to shake things up. Get ready for a wild ride.
-You must digest what you have learned and experienced. Make sure to integrate everything before moving.

*DO: "I am strong" affirmations

THE BITE
She walked in like she'd done before, poised, polished, practiced. She was someone the world recognized. A public face with a private ache. Her energy had changed, but not in the way people assume when someone returns from the limelight. She had picked up more wounds. The invisible kind. The ones you can't name, but you feel in your nervous system.
Like clockwork her father and auntie come through. They didn't rush to say anything, they just stood beside her. Protective. Familiar. They didn't always come with words. Sometimes they just came to hold the space.
Spirit showed me that she needed healing. The kind of deep spiritual recalibration that comes when you've given too much of your light to rooms that weren't built to hold it. Fame had its cost. The image she had to keep

up demanded pieces of her that she never agreed to give. And yet, she had survived. Still soft because of her faith. Still open to Spirit. I placed her on my medicine blanket, and I could feel how much she had been through in the world she lived in, scrutinized, adored, used, misunderstood. During prayer, she didn't cry. She didn't collapse. She just exhaled.

Weeks later, she told me something had happened. Someone took advantage of her again. Financially. She saw it coming but ignored her gut. Her words were not bitter. They were calm. She said, "Veronica, I knew. I saw it. And I didn't listen. But now I know better."

Her voice didn't tremble like before. It carried weight now, not the weight of sorrow, but of self.

She was no longer just surviving. She was watching, choosing, waiting. There was power in her stillness. Like something with teeth had finally remembered its bite.

GREEN GRASSHOPPPER

-Trust that you will receive everything that you need to finish your project. Let Go!

-You must go ahead and do it, you do not have to know the outcome.

→ Something that you have been avoiding -largescale- will change in direction.

- Relationship /advance in career or transition within yourself

*Remember to move with intent and a healthy mindset.

→ An opportunity will come that is going to help you in completing your goals.

• Remember to pursue what your gut is telling you – listen to your inner voice.

-It is time to play big, you are about to enter a new state of a healthy life and restoration making it easy for you to find a spiritual connection to the universe.

-Remember, stay in the present moment.

-You have the freedom to break free from limitations.

-Trust your intuition.

-Incorporate nature into your routine.

-Death Rebirth

PRAY FOR: Hope, growth, abundance, good luck
DO: Chakra meditations

THE PITCH

She booked a cleansing session, but Spirit always reveals the truth. She did not come for healing. She came for answers, fast ones. Financial ones. She wanted her future read like a stock forecast. And when

Spirit did not deliver dollar signs, she lost interest. Her energy shifted from curiosity to calculation.

Twenty minutes into her hour session she switched. Suddenly, the cleanse became a pitch.

Her words were sweet, but her actions revealed it all, she was there to reach Ivana. To reach her brand, her light, her power. She did not want guidance, she wanted access. She wanted to insert her ideas into Ivana's path, hoping they would become profitable. But what she did not understand is that this path is sacred. This space is protected. We do not hustle Spirit. We do not barter with blessings. I let the clock tick but stayed connected to God.

Because I know Holy Spirit sees my heart, and my only intent was to help her grow. To cleanse the energy weighing her down. To remind her that there is a better way to live, a freer way.

But she did not want the freedom that comes from growth. She wanted shortcuts. She did not see the medicine, only the means. And that's okay.

Some souls do not mind repeating cycles. Some souls choose to return again and again to lessons they could have completed in one visit. Spirit offered her abundance, rebirth, good luck but she did not want the stillness it takes to receive.

The Green Grasshopper brings that message: Leap. Let go. Trust. But she didn't leap, she lobbied.

I whispered a blessing over her as she left. Because healing does not stop just because someone doesn't take the offer. Spirit plants the seed anyway. One day, maybe she will let it grow.

PHEASANT

-Today will be a day of knowing when to express your opinions and when to let others do the talking.

-Remember that you have untapped creative passions that are burning deep within you. These passions are calling for exploration. Know that anything that you start right now that feeds those passions will be endlessly productive for you.

-Do a little bit of self-evolution and make sure you are enjoying the pleasures of life and the beauty that surrounds you.

-Take time to discover new erotic experiences and practice good fellowship.

*Happiness is right there for you to embrace. Enjoy all the beautiful things around you. Believe that you are worthy of all of this and of your success.

->Air – You can turn your thoughts to dreams, higher awareness, personal aspirations, clairvoyance and clairaudience.

-Remain open to fresh experiences and people.

-When you doubt your skills tell yourself, "Enough with the insecurities.

*The power of attraction is vibrant in your life if you stick to your guns. You can draw the most energy you need in your life using your will.

*Take your vitamins!

*Stop focusing so much on big missions that you overlook the small miracles every day.

*You don't have to fly the flag for everyone, only the right people.

PRAY FOR: ability to use the law of attraction, abundance, creativity, sexuality, passion, flirtation

<u>BLOCKS AND CLEANSE</u>
Sacral Chakra
EAT: More Orange foods
REPEAT: Centering Affirmations
DO: yin yoga – warrior, goddess pose, low lunge, pigeon pose, stretches, spend time in baths / water
CREATE: new hobby
Root Chakra
DO: Grounding
DRINK: cinnamon tea

YOU ARE ENOUGH

I had a client who came for a reading. She was a model who had graced the covers of magazines, the kind of woman who made the world pause when she walked into a room. To the outside world, she looked like she had it all: fame, beauty, admiration. But when she came to see me, Spirit showed me something different. She wanted more. Not more fame or more followers but more meaning, more fire, more soul. She was secretly ashamed of how she judged herself for not "having it all together" by a certain age. She felt like time was catching up with her, and the glow that had lit up her younger years was dimming under the pressure of expectations. During our session, her father came through first, his voice firm but warm, urging her to stop comparing herself to others. Then her grandmother showed up, proud, protective. Her aunt was there too wise, nurturing, and she told her she would help guide her through a secret project she was too afraid to begin. Lastly, a cousin came with a simple message for his father, her uncle, something only they would understand. It was love, pure and unspoken.

I laid her down on my medicine blanket and led her into guided meditation. As she sank into stillness, Spirit wrapped around her like velvet. I did an egg cleanse to help unblock her sacral Chakra, heavy with self-doubt and the buried shame of "not being enough." I handed her the egg and told her: "Go into the forest. Throw it far. Make sure you never see it again."

The Pheasant was her guide that day. It reminded her to fall back in love with beauty, with life, with the pleasure of small things. To flirt with her passions again. To remember that creative fire does not belong to the young it belongs to the brave. And she, more than anything, needed to remember she was worthy of pleasure, of joy, of becoming someone new at any age.

EARTHWORM 𝟤𝟫

-Look deep within yourself to discover your real strengths and potential.

-Do not run away from your problems, it is time to start dealing with them.

- Reevaluate your life and improve in areas where you are not accomplishing more.

-You are harmoniously balanced with yourself.

-You are not alone even when you feel small and insignificant.

-Do not be afraid to be in the garden, around trees and planting. Acknowledge nature and its integral role in your life.

-Trust your emotions and act on them. Trust those feelings you are having about something or someone.

-Take things slowly and carefully - taking one step at a time and avoid rushing into things this will enable you to see opportunities and absorb the experiences surrounding you.

-Don't be an open book to everyone! Right now, keep things to yourself - this is especially important for you to avoid disappointments.

-Get ready for new beginnings and changes.

-You matter and your efforts make a difference.

-Shake off your past so you can move forward.

-Remain focused on exploring your true self.

PRAY FOR: Rebirth, fertility, restoration, prosperity

HE ONLY CAME TO KISS HIS FOREHEAD

I had a man come in for a session. He said he wanted his money blessed. Said it just like that, like it was a business transaction. But Spirit does not work that way. I sat with him. I prayed over his palms. And the second I touched his energy; I felt a wave of sadness rush through me. But it wasn't loud or dramatic, it was quiet love. It was forgiveness.

It was someone on the other side saying, "It is okay. Let him be seen." His grandfather came in, not with a message, not with words. Just walked up in Spirit and kissed him softly on the forehead, then left. I remember thinking how gentle that was. How rare. It did not feel like a performance. It felt real.

Then Spirit guided me to do a deep cleanse. I felt his spirit shedding things he did not even speak aloud. Guilt, shame, fear of failure. He was carrying a lot, and for a moment I truly believed that he was ready to heal. But time has a way of revealing the truth. A few weeks later, he showed who he really was.

A manipulative liar who tried to scam us. He tried to twist things, take advantage, taint our name, and poison the water after he drank from it. And I remember sitting with the feeling of betrayal. The embarrassment. The anger. But mostly the confusion. How did I not see it coming? I am a psychic. A healer. I am supposed to know.

I went into prayer and asked my God, "Why didn't you show me?" And the answer came like a whisper: Because even the tricksters are worthy of healing.

Not everything we do is about protecting ourselves from people's darkness.

Sometimes it is about showing love even when people do not know how to receive it.

Even when they lie. Even when they take. The lesson was not about him.

It was about me. My ability to still love. To still serve. To give without losing my soul. That is the part of the work that nobody sees, the heartbreak that happens when you give your gift in good faith and someone spits on it. But guess what? Even that gets transmuted. In my space, there is no punishment, no revenge, no judgment. Only love. Only lessons. Only God.

part 3

At this stage in my journey with spirit animal communication, something began to shift, spirit animal messages started coming in shorter phrases. Almost like spiritual abbreviations, the way people text using shortcuts like "LOL" or "BRB." At first, I wasn't sure what was happening. Was I missing something? But I realized it was the opposite. Spirit was trusting me more. I was being shown that I no longer needed to hold onto every single word like I used to. I didn't need passages to guide the mood or shape the energy of each reading. I didn't need to be told exactly how to proceed. It wasn't less powerful it was just more direct. Spirit no longer needed to explain everything word for word, because I had grown. Those short phrases now sparked full understanding in my heart. It was like Spirit saying, "You already know, trust your psychic abilities, all of them." And around this same time, another level of understanding opened up. Spirit animals began to show me how to work more with Chakras not in a mechanical or surface-level way, but intuitively, energetically, and spiritually. They began revealing which energy centers were calling for attention, how different animals were connected to certain Chakras, and how their presence could help clear, activate, or restore balance. The more I listened, the more I saw that Chakra healing and animal medicine were not separated. They were speaking to each other, working together to guide people back into harmony. In this part of my book, I use spirit animal messages as guidance, not dependency. They show up to help me answer questions with more clarity, but I don't lean on them the way I once did. And yes, I still call them in. I still honor their presence. I still invite them to help me hold space when I'm calling forward someone's loved ones. But they've become a trusted tool, not a lifeline.

RAVEN

*Sirus

-Unconditional love

-Make your wellbeing priority at work or home.
You cannot be a good friend to others without having the same relationship with yourself.

-Minister /metaphysical teacher

-Remember to pause and consider your battles.

-Remember it is ok to stop and have fun *burn out*

Tune in and Live in the moment

PRAY FOR: family, adaptability, devotion, bravery, insightfulness and personal purpose

BLOCKS AND CLEANSE

Heart Chakra

DRINK: Jasmine Tea

REPEAT: "I AM WORTHY" Affirmations

What spirit animal told me my client was suffering from:
Loneliness, insecurity, hurt, unable to receive love - walls, shutting down emotionally, resentment

SOUL SESSION

Through my computer screen, I saw my client, shoulders sunken with the kind of weariness that doesn't come from just a lack of sleep it was soul deep. The kind of tired you carry when your light has been dimmed for too long. What unfolded was far beyond either of our expectations.

As soon as she spoke, I felt the shift. The usual flow of words softened into a stillness, and I felt myself drift gently. My consciousness moved beyond the room and

I was guided to "leave" my body and through remote viewing, I was shown her store in real time. I described what I saw. The layout, the shelves, the season's latest collection, even the small details. She confirmed it all.

Spirit walked me through its corners, the light fixtures, and even the feel of the neighborhood. Holy Spirit began to speak. I became the vessel, receiving clear direction for her business, insight that would reignite her path and bless the other dream she had once loved. Spirit gave her comfort to know that she was not alone, that she still had that fire, to go after all of her dreams. But it didn't stop there. Spirit allowed me to feel the heavy heartbeats she carried. The resented wounds and family burdens. The walls she'd built around her heart were thick, and they were silent. She wasn't just tired. She was alone and guarded. Spirit reminded her of her soul mission and of the fire she'd buried underneath years of showing up for everyone except herself.

Later, I visited her store in person. And just like in the vision, it stood as I had seen it down to the smallest details. I blessed the space anointing the front door, setting intentions, and speaking life back into the heart of her dream. That moment was a confirmation, for me. Spirit sees. Spirit knows. And spirit never lets us walk alone.

HUMMINGBIRD

-Time to grab on to joy as quickly as you can
- It is time for you to pursue your dreams more aggressively, by doing this you will make them a reality.
-You must believe that you can manifest them now. Stop waiting.
-Know that you can go anywhere you need to go, the only obstacle in your way is yourself.
-Opportunities are manifesting quickly right now, seize them as fast as you can before they are gone.
-Enjoy the simple things in life.
-You are long past due for me time.
- Remember it's never too late to explore ways to create a new reality.
-Stop finding purpose for those that won't blossom.
*Don't be afraid of detours.
*Don't be so in your thoughts

PRAY FOR: Inspiration and renewal, freedom, hope, mood, communication

BLOCKS AND CLEANSE
Heart Chakra
WEAR: green clothes and crystals
DRINK: peppermint tea
EAT: green foods
REPEAT: "I am worthy" affirmations
DO: open chest exercises / yoga

Solar Plexus Chakra
WEAR: yellow clothes
CARRY: tiger's eye stone in your pocket
DRINK: Rosemary, bergamot, chamomile teas

What spirit animal told me my client was suffering from: Fatigue, stomach ulcers, indigestion, liver and kidney problems, bloating, lack of self-confidence, stuck in anger and isolation, grudges, and fear of intimacy

THE HUMMINGBIRD'S WHISPER

She came to me with questions about life, purpose, and the next steps on her path. A young woman with an undeniable strength both in business and in spirit but something was off. She was thriving in her work yet neglecting the part of herself that made her truly powerful.

As we spoke, I saw it her energy was restless, her heart weighed down. She was pouring herself into work, into others, but not into herself. She had put off her own growth, her own dreams, believing there would always be time later. I delivered the spirit animal reading in psychic detail. The hummingbird reminded her that opportunities were fleeting, that detours weren't failures but new paths waiting to unfold. She had the ability to create anything she desired if only she allowed herself to believe it.

She listened, absorbing every word.

Before she left, I guided her through a heart and solar plexus cleanse, lifting the blocks that had dimmed her light. As she walked away, I could already feel the shift. The hummingbird had done its work, now, it was up to her to take flight.

COCKROACH

*Survivor
-When you get the door of opportunity and it won't open, look for ways in and make your own way.
→Use every opportunity life is offering to you.
-You are hiding your true self from others get into the light and let people see your true self
Limelight
-Share your ideas with friends and colleagues.
-Problem? Talk about it to someone *(seek counseling)
-Watch what you eat.
-You are the brain behind big ideas but you let others get the praise.
–Know that you are smart, talented, hardworking, and goal oriented.
Community
-Where there is a will there is a way.
• Live in the present moment.
-Where are you putting your energy?
-What are you doing to use your power for building the future?
-Do you choose fear over courage?
 -Consider your decisions.
-Remember to trust your senses.
*Focus on your diet-healthy!
-Know that you will be ok.
-Change or move?

THE WARNING

The cockroach isn't a spirit animal many would welcome, but its message is one of resilience and survival. When it appeared for my young client, I knew it carried something important. As I tuned in, visions of his future unfolded. His business had the potential to thrive, yet a storm loomed. A colleague, weighed down by addiction, was steering things off course. If my client continued to trust him blindly, everything he had built would crumble.

Then came the vision of his girlfriend, her heart open, waiting. She wasn't just seeking more love; she was seeking commitment. Marriage was on her mind, a future with him. But was he ready?

I delivered the messages with care, letting him sit with the truth. The cockroach reminded him that survival isn't just about endurance, it's about adaptation. He had choices to make, and his future depended on them. I hope he listened to his own intuition and did what was best.

MONARCH BUTTERFLY

-Transformation

-Old and unhealthy-purge

*Time (use it wisely)

-Life has been stagnant

-Stay true to your voice.

* Do not give your information away or that which is given to you in trust.

-Release those things that weigh heavy on your heart.

• Remember to laugh.

*Self-evaluation - What is holding you back?

-You are a leader and healer - heal yourself

*The undertakings are temporary.

*Keep your senses open, don't brush off your hunches.

-Don't be afraid of falling short or rejection.

PRAY FOR: old mindset, unhealthy patterns, self-respect

BLOCKS AND CLEANSE

Third Eye Chakra

WEAR: Purple clothes, crystals

EAT: purple diet

DO: yoga- child's pose

REPEAT: affirmations to strengthen your intuition

What spirit animal told me my client was suffering from: Headaches, dizziness, sinus, hearing, eyesight, memory loss, anxiety, tension in the brow area, and worriedness

After the cleansing a final message came through from spirit council: You are the master of all synchronicities. Know in your heart that all doors are open wide.

MRS. SYLVIA

As I prepared for my next reading on my gratitude walk, the monarch butterfly appeared. Its wings, a striking contrast of black and orange, fluttering with purpose. I knew then that transformation was at the heart of this session. My client, a young woman, came to me carrying the weight of heartbreak. She was in the thick of a painful breakup, lost in a storm of unanswered questions and betrayal she could feel but hadn't yet proven. As soon as we connected, a presence stepped forward, an unexpected spirit, not a family member but her grandmother's dear friend, Sylvia.

Sylvia didn't know my client in life, yet she came through with warmth, wisdom, and an undeniable sense of purpose. She had a message to deliver. Gently, she guided my client toward the truth she had been avoiding. He was unfaithful, she confirmed, and in that moment, I could see it too through remote viewing. Flashes of dishonesty, moments hidden in the shadows. My client's face shifted from sadness to a quiet relief. She had felt it all along, but now she had the confirmation she needed to let go.

But Sylvia wasn't just here to expose the past, she was here to help shape the future. She spoke to my client about her life direction, her education, the dreams she had put on hold. Time is precious. Use it wisely. Don't let this heartbreak hold you back. The monarch's energy echoed this, reminding her that transformation comes from release.

As we moved through the session, I guided her through a cleanse, lifting the heavy energy that clouded her intuition. By the end, her spirit felt lighter. And as she left, I saw it in her eyes, clarity, strength, and the first glimpse of the wings she was about to spread.

LIZARD

-Regeneration, Rebirth, Renewal

-Clear your head.

-Positive mindset

-Break cycles

       → emotional cycles

*Remember this current setback is temporary.

* Exciting opportunity ahead!

*Pay close attention to your intuition – people rely on it.

-Meditate – Astral Travel

-Self-care is very important right now.

<u>BLOCKS AND CLEANSE</u>

Sacral Chakra

EAT: orange foods

REPEAT: "I honor and respect my choices" affirmations

DO: low plunge / yoga – start a new hobby

What spirit animal told me my client was suffering from: Depression, anxiety, harsh menstrual cramps, UTI, lower back pain, feeling closed off and uncomfortable with her body, feelings of shame regarding sexual drive

NO FIGHTING

During my daily meditation, I was in my spirit animal garden when suddenly, a new animal appeared to join the rest, it was a Lizard. So, I knew immediately that its presence carried a message for my next client. She was a young woman in the middle of a painful divorce, struggling with anger, fear, and lingering love for her soon-to-be ex-husband. He was making the process difficult fighting over money, alienating her, and leaving her feeling lost. She wanted guidance on what to do next.

As I connected, her grandmother came through with a strong and loving presence. She reassured her that she wasn't alone and that peace, not conflict, would bring her the best outcome. She confirmed details my client had told no one. Her plans for a new home and her thoughts about hiring a different attorney. This validation gained her trust, and she listened as her grandmother guided her on how to move forward without resentment.

The session was powerful. Spirit led me to cleanse her sacral Chakra, helping her release feelings of shame and guilt. By the end, her energy had shifted. It was lighter, clearer, and more at peace with the path ahead.

WORM

-Remember that things can still improve regardless of how bad the situation has gone.

*Utilize life's opportunities.

*True self - Get into the light - Let people see your true self.

-Communication

- Work -sharing of ideas

→talk problems through

*Health- watch what you are eating

** Survivor

- Where are you putting your energy?

• Consider your decisions.

↳ fear? give it up

-Blockage -Stuck-

-You are at the edge of a huge change in your life – know that wherever this adventure ends up

– You will be ok.

PRAY FOR Properties, direction, communication

THE WORMS HELP UNBURYING HER VOICE

During a reading with an older woman, a vision appeared, one so heavy and delicate that I had to approach it with care.

I saw her as a child, carrying a silent pain she had never spoken of. She had been hurt sexually as a child and had never given herself the space to heal. That wound followed her into adulthood, shaping the life she settled for. A lifelong marriage built not on love, but on survival. She had stayed because it was safe, at least in the material sense. But emotionally she had been trapped.

Her husband's abuse, his control, even his demands over her body, had kept her bound in fear. His constant need for deviant sexual behavior was causing her harm. I asked for help in delivering this truth without causing her shame. And then, her parents came through. Their presence was gentle yet firm, filled with the love she had always deserved. They spoke of hope, of a life still waiting for her beyond the prison she had come to accept. They helped me guide her through the spirit animal's message, reminding her that no matter how long she had felt stuck, change was still possible.

For the first time, she allowed herself to see beyond fear. To consider what freedom might feel like. The weight she had carried for a lifetime began to lift. And in that moment, she was no longer just surviving. She was ready to live.

MOTH

-Death, Rebirth, and Transformation

*Suppressed -the feeling like others take advantage of you

*Struggling with how you deal with significant changes in life.

-Hiding emotional vulnerabilities

-Try to embrace transformation with grace.

->It is time to sooth, calm and assure your soul.

• Feeling unattractive (deep wounds)

-Lustful foolishness

-You are hiding your true self but overexposed - showing the wrong people your weaknesses

-Remember sometimes it's easy to have something distract you. A "bright light" calls out. But it is time to adjust your course toward a safer haven.

-Beware and in control with your lunar vibrations, meditation and self-discovery this in turn will leave a clearer head particularly in matters of romance love.

*Self-esteem

- Energize your sensuality

- Compatible partner

Warning! Stop hiding things from yourself in the shadow of darkness.

-Look inward and be honest.

- We see that you are optimistic always even through all your life's darkness.

-Remember to smile when the night seems to last forever.

*You can attract attention with little effort - don't worry - don't fuss - the circumstances and people you want will land at your feet.
*The law of attraction abides in your DNA.
→Sacred dance←
-Stay true, dig deep, don't accept surface appearances.
• We hear you and see you, how you feel, you lost sight of your passion and feel like all light has gone out of your life. Turn away from things that no longer serve you -> move forward.
-We celebrate the true you!
-Enjoy your strengths and talents and work on the rest as you go.

A LIGHT IN THE DARKNESS

My client came to me searching for answers. She was navigating an open relationship with her spouse and questioning the direction of her business. There was uncertainty around her, like she was standing at the edge of a decision but unsure whether to take the next step. As I connected with her energy, something unexpected happened. A presence filled the space. It was an older couple, warm and familiar, but not her biological family. Their energy was deeply parental, protective, filled with love. I hesitated for a moment before asking, "Do you know why an Asian couple would come into your reading as your parents?"
She looked at me, surprised. "My friend's parents. They were Asian. I used to call them Mom and Dad."
That was it. They had come through to remind her that she was not alone. They knew she was at a crossroads, and they wanted her to trust herself. The contrast was

striking, an African American woman being embraced and guided by an Asian couple in spirit. It was a reminder that love, and connection transcend race, background, and even this physical life.

Holy Spirit guided me to pray over her body, focusing on her self-worth and balance. There was something about her presence that made it difficult to read her fully. Some clients are like that.

But I didn't need to know how she was feeling. That wasn't my role.

I am only the messenger, the liaison between the spiritual and the physical world. I deliver what is given to me and trust that it will serve its purpose.

As the session came to an end, I could sense a shift, not necessarily a resolution, but a moment of pause. Whether she felt better or not, only she knew. But the moth had given her something to reflect on. The choice, as always, was hers.

BUTTERFLY

-Massive Transformation

-Embrace changes in your body, emotions, and environment.

-This physical transformation of energy is taking root and expanding around you in ways that you can't imagine and that will surprise you.

-Release any expectations you have about the outcome of this change. Do not try to control it.

*Keep your faith.

*Move-dance- bring color into your life.

-It is time for personal growth and greater awareness of your mental, physical and spiritual self.

→ Release the old to embrace the new you.

*Go back to the little things that make you happy.

-Live in the moment.

• Self-care- Take time in your own home.

*Know that your ancestors remain in your life to help guide the way.

• Friends -use your intuition

-Step out of your circle to gain what is lacking. Be creative.

->Transit → spiritual awakening /self-discovery

PRAY FOR: Happiness, hope, abundance, health, education

TRANSFORMATION THROUGH LOVE

My client was a woman carrying both grief and questions, unsure of how to move forward. As I connected with her energy, I immediately felt the presence of her late husband. Then, his spirit came through strong, filled with love and reassurance.

He spoke of their son, their grandkids, and the plans they had once dreamed of together. His words were gentle, but they carried a purpose. He wanted her to know that he was still with her, watching over their family. Then, he mentioned something unexpected: his ashes and honeybees. I wasn't sure what it meant, but as soon as I spoke the words, I saw the recognition in her eyes.

Sometimes, messages from spirit don't need to be explained. They land exactly where they're meant to. Holy Spirit guided me to cleanse her energy, helping her realign with hope and abundance. The shift was subtle, but it was there. Then before I closed in prayer, he came through again to tell her that he wanted her to embrace life again, to find joy in the little things, to release control over the future and allow herself to be. The grief would never fully disappear, but neither would his love.

MOSQUITO

-Keep moving forward and manifesting your destiny. These little irritants that are affecting you are simply temporary.

-Protect your creative projects and yourself from those who wish to undermine your goals.

*Be aware of jealous and fearful individuals around you, nervous that you will be better than them.

→ Work and home environment will change

* You are put on notice regarding relationships decisions. Deal with the issues before the relationship can deepen or thrive.

->Clairsentience - the ability to sense vibrations in one's environment – research – practice it

→Clear your emotions = submerge yourself in water

•Disturbed by someone or something

-Stop burying things you should overcome.

-You are paying attention to dismissive superficial matters. Use your energy in better ways.

-Never release your will power when nagged incessantly.

• Look long and hard at the places where you spend a lot of time and the company you keep, are they healthy or sucking you dry?

-Beware, toxic environments are beginning to feel normal.

• Make list of what needs to change.

-Pay attention - What you receive, what you give out, what you desire, and what you block.

• Take time on your actions and reactions. What are you giving off?

*Remain attentive to boundaries and limits set by others. Don't rush in with ideas or aids if boundaries have been set.

-Don't let your drive turn into opportunistic behavior. Seek energy exchanges instead. Give receive repeat.

-Don't focus – if everything seems out of whack.

! Use water for inner emotional healing and soul searching, some of what you'll find will sting but you will come out healthier.

BLOCKS AND CLEANSE
Sacral Chakra – for emotions

EAT: orange foods

WEAR: orange colors (lower part of the body – abdomen)

REPEAT: Positive Affirmations

 "I have everything I need to create the life that I desire."

"I am safe and grounded."

"I release anxiety and fear."

"I am at home in my body."

What spirit animal told me my client was suffering from: Depression, UTI, lower back pain, feeling closed off and uncomfortable with her body, feelings of shame and problems with her female organs

SOUL CONTRACT
Before my client even entered the room, I could already feel her grief moving through my body. The sensation was so intense I had to pause. I had a full hysterectomy and haven't felt pain in my ovaries in years, yet it was my ovaries that felt extreme pain.

During the reading, a young male soul came through, radiating peace and love. He gently revealed himself as the child she had chosen not to bring into the world, a pregnancy from her early twenties that she chose to end with an abortion. She had never shared with anyone. His presence was so kind and compassionate. He wasn't there to judge her. He was there to comfort her.

He explained that their agreement had been made long before either of them incarnated. That his brief existence had purpose, even if it never reached the physical world. He reminded her that souls do not measure love in time spent on Earth. Her actions were not betrayal, they were part of the journey they had mapped together.

He also offered healing for her heartache around relationships, particularly with men, and her struggles with fertility. She was stunned.

She hadn't expected that level of insight, especially from a soul she'd hidden from the world.

Months later, I saw her again. She was glowing. She had become pregnant. Her energy was softer, lighter. I could tell that the reading had helped her release a weight she didn't even know she was carrying.

Sometimes we don't get to see the full circle, but in this case, God allowed me to witness the transformation.

PIG

-Your life is about to flourish.

-It is time to connect to Earth Element /Mother Gaia.

-Are you trying to find treasures in life?

-Have you forgotten how to have fun?

-Find life's treasures while maintaining your playful spirit!

-New networking leads are coming now that you are secure.

-Stay in gratitude and share your wealth.

-A period of quiet self-awareness continues so continue to tap into your ingenuity so you can turn a dime without falling over.

->Make the most of the situation in front of you, if you're not being nourished like you desire, then move on forward not backward.

->You are blessed with luck and with money so remember you are a person for whom creating your reality comes easily.

*Fertility in business and career

*Know that your throat Chakra is blessed-your voice will always be distinctive and clear.

- Beware of too many options and over stimulation.

-Have courage.

*Learn to calm yourself in anger.

*Let mother Earth remove toxins in our life stemming from irritating people and situations.

-Know that you are blessed with a teacher, a companion who will bring you joy at the perfect time to protect you against greed, gluttony, and ego centricity.

-You are blessed with the gifts of reasoning, thoughtfulness, fairness, attentiveness and security.
*Move forward!
• Remember you have what it takes to flourish in life!
-Keep friends that influence your life positively

BLOCKS AND CLEANSE
Root Chakra
WEAR: Red clothes, crystals
EAT: Red diet
DRINK: Schisandra Berry, red clover, dandelion tea, burdock tea
SMELL: Oregano
DO: yoga- lotus pose and child's pose
CHANT- LAM

What spirit animal told me my client was suffering from: Worriedness, anemia, problems at the base of the spine, was in survival mode, lacked courage

THE COLLECTIVVE ILLUSION

When my client arrived, I knew instantly something wasn't right. As I opened our session in prayer, the energy shifted quickly into a soul reading. I was shown the physical pain she was carrying not just emotional, but deep in her body.

After the reading, she revealed that she had filled her body with substances trying to mold herself into someone more "acceptable," more "desired." But what once felt empowering had become a silent burden. Her body was now calling out for help.

She had been pulled into the same pressure I've seen so many women face trying to look a certain way. She, like several of my other clients before her, had filled her body with things to change her shape: cheeks, lips, butt, breasts. She had been drawn into the collective illusion of beauty, one shaped by external validation, social media, and silent suffering and she needed more than prayer.

As I prayed, Spirit showed me that she was in danger and this wasn't something I could energetically remove. It needed urgent physical healing.

This was hard for me. I always want to be the healer, to fix it with energy, love, and Holy Spirit. But sometimes, the message is clear: this person needs a doctor. She needs medical help. And that doesn't mean the spiritual part failed.

Her story, and others like her, showed me something important. Sometimes the choices we regret are part of the journey. The healing might not happen how we expect, but that doesn't mean healing isn't happening. My part was just one piece of her path, and it mattered. Spirit reminded me of that.

Not every session ends with a big transformation you can see. But I know that moment planted something inside her, and inside me. We're both learning. We're both healing.

(As a psychic healer, I believe that true beauty begins in the spirit, but I also honor the things that help us feel radiant in our skin; I use Botox, fillers, etc. I believe that all things in that realm when used with intention, love, and care can uplift your confidence and that becomes part of your healing, too.) ☺

DRAGONFLY

-Massive Transformation
-Embrace changes in your emotional environment and with your emotional body.
↳ Mental, physical, and spiritual rhythms
-Release expectations and control.
Faith
- Move / stagnant / dance
*Remember you are on a long soul journey.
* Balance and Harmony
- Let go of your burdens

BLOCKS AND CLEANSE
Solar Plexus Chakra
WEAR: yellow and golden clothes, crystals
DO: warrior pose, spinal twists
DRINK: bergamot, rose Mary, chamomile
EAT: Pumpkin
CHANT: RAM

What spirit animal told me my client was suffering from: diabetes, arthritis, poor digestion, gas, aches, nerve pain, weight gain, low self-esteem

FAVORITE AUNT

Walking along the shore in Long Beach, I felt the warmth of the sun and the cool ocean breeze. I enjoyed my gratitude walk, my moments of peace and a dragonfly caught my eye. Its delicate, translucent wings shimmered against the backdrop of soft rolling waves, darting and hovering as if guiding me. I knew then: this was a sign. A message was coming.

I followed its flight, watching how it danced with the wind, until just before it vanished, I noticed a woman approaching me. Every movement she made felt significant; it was spirit imprinting her into my memory. I didn't know why yet, but I knew I would. In my next reading, the dragonfly, lead me back to the image of the woman on the beach. And then, spirit moved. Her aunt stepped forward, gentle, strong, and full of love. She spoke through me with ease, as if no time had passed since she had last held her niece. She had died of breast cancer, but in this moment, she was here. Both in California where I sat, and in Europe, where my client watched me through her computer screen.

My client's eyes filled with emotion, but not with sorrow, with warmth, and with love. She spoke to her aunt like she was right there, laughing and reminiscing, just like they did when she was alive.

And then, the details came. Messages of guidance, life plans, decisions she had been weighing on her heart. Even small, unexpected things, a sign to move forward with fixing her car, and the confirmation that her daughter's dental work would be taken care of. The dragonfly knew. It had led me exactly where I needed to be.

BEAR

-Quiet, Privacy
-Has life lost a bit of its sweetness?
-Rest and Relaxation
*It is time to trust your instincts and let go of all that blocks your path.
-Higher self is preparing you for a position of leadership
-Know that you are protected (situation)
*Know that you have been provided with strength in times when you feel weak or helpless.
*Stay connected to yourself.
-Accept an authoritative role not only in your life but that of others.
-baby-
-Find your truth and live it with your humor and honor.
> balance<
- Wisdom, strength, and healing
-Don't forget to treat yourself to the goodness you treat others with.
-Shadow work
-Keep an open mind- find new knowledge in experiences
-Remain flexible, teachable and playful, curious and affectionate
*Connect with the forest.

BLOCKS AND CLEANSE
Throat Chakra
EAT: Blue foods, basil, mushrooms
WEAR: blue clothes, crystals
DO: yoga- shoulder stand, neck circles fish pose
DRINK: peppermint tea

-Write Letters to loved ones
-Mak phone calls to friends and family
-Listen to 320 Hz
-Sing

What spirit animal told me my client was suffering from: Laryngitis, sore throat, tension, body pain especially in shoulders and knees, thyroid, lymph system, pituitary gland, teeth, gums, nose, ears, sinus, respiratory

A BEAR'S HUG

During an online reading, a mother's presence surrounded me. It was strong, protective, and filled with love. She had passed, but she came through with a message for her daughter, my client.

My client was an elderly woman, carrying the weight of an exhausting real estate battle with her baby brother. The fight had stretched on for years, draining her spirit, leaving her body tense and in pain. Her mother's love was gentle but firm: Let go. Stand in your strength, but do not let this break you.

As I connected deeper, I felt the bear's presence in the aching in her knees, the tension in her shoulders, and the unspoken words caught in her throat. This battle had silenced her in ways she hadn't even realized. She was a woman who had spent her life caring for others, yet she had forgotten how to care for herself.

Her mother urged her to soften, to trust that she was protected, to remember that she was stronger than she felt. The bear's quiet wisdom mirrored her mother's message: You have the strength to lead, but you must also allow yourself to heal. As the session ended, I guided her through a deep energy cleanse. The tension lifted, her voice grew lighter, and for the first time in a long while, she allowed herself to breathe.

The bear had come to remind her: true strength is not just in fighting battles, but in knowing when to release them.

LLAMA

-Remember say what you mean and mean what you say.

-Communication

-Bite tongue -swallow words

-Throat Chakra -feeling stuck

? How much is on your plate right now? It is time to get rid of burdens. Are you taking on way too much?

*Burn out

-Self-image pride -don't let yourself be mistreated

→ Haunting spirit

→Lost dream or goal, it's time to go after it. Don't rush but move towards it!

• Release weighty emotions - block

-Trust your own path.

-Repeat "Royalty Affirmations" daily.

*Focus on you!

PRAY FOR: Confidence, adaptability, balance, community, diligence, courage, patience, stamina, focus

TRUST WHAT YOU KNOW

During an online spirit animal reading, the llama came in with calm but serious energy. This wasn't going to be a light session. Llama shows up when it's time to carry weight, get clear, and move steady through challenges, especially when it comes to work and leadership.

As I settled into the session, I began to remote view into my client's space. I could feel right away this reading wasn't about love or family. It was all work-related. I saw his office, his desk, the energy around his business and one woman stood out in the middle of it all.

Spirit showed me everything: her energy was heavy, off, and dark. She wasn't just negative; she was stealing from him. I described her to him: her role, her appearance, even her office location inside his building. He nodded. He already knew something was wrong, just needed spiritual confirmation.

Holy Spirit didn't guide me to do a deep cleanse. Just prayer. That's all that was needed to seal the truth and give him clarity.

This reading reminded me of something powerful: when negative energy is given space, it doesn't just affect our emotions. It can block blessings, mess with our money, cloud our judgment, and quietly wear down our self-esteem. All without us realizing what's happening.

Some doors need to be closed right away. And sometimes we already know but Spirit steps in to remind us to trust what we feel and take action.

BLACK EAGLE
-Transformation and change
-Face your fears and make the most of any situation.
* Take on a more prominent leadership role and own your authority.
-Time to stand up for yourself.
*Fresh start
-Use your leadership abilities for humanity not for self-glorification.
-May relate to work or hobbies: arts, drama, science
-Use air / wind to cleanse yourself, to feel freedom, and open up to communication

PRAY FOR: Wisdom

BLOCKS AND CLEANSE
Solar Plexus Chakra
WEAR: yellow clothing, tiger's eye
DO: yoga- lion's pose, warriors pose
DRINK: bergamot, chamomile tea

What spirit animal told me my client was suffering from: Stomach issues, problems with weight, diabetes, gastrointestinal, heartburn, poor digestion, lack of direction, self-esteem issues, over thinker, anxiety / Great feelings of incompleteness without someone to share love, ideas, wealth, or work

THE MAN WHO SMILED
He came to me as many do with kind eyes, soft voice, and a soul tightly wrapped in silence. A man who carried light in his smile and shadows in his bones. He asked for a cleanse. He said he wanted to feel "lighter."

But the moment I placed my hands on his body during the opening prayer, I felt a wave of sorrow so thick it nearly pulled me under.

It wasn't just emotional pain. It was ancestral, coded into his blood. A grief so old it had grown quiet. My soul cried out to his in a language older than words.

He hid his sadness so well. Buried in his art, his children, his stories about love and family. But I could see it in the air between us. Like smoke you can't touch but still smell. I could feel it buzzing beneath my skin. He smiled as he asked questions, as he tried to distract me with kindness and curiosity. But his organs screamed to mine. His DNA burned like fire; I could feel the heat.

Spirit stopped me before I could speak. A vision had come, but I wasn't allowed to share it yet. It's rare that I'm given futures like this. Rarer still when I'm told to wait. I saw how deeply he adored his wife, how she was the missing piece in his puzzle. The love he gave her was unconditional, pure, sacred. But she didn't want it. Not anymore. Her distance left him unraveling in silence, questioning his manhood, his worth, his purpose. He tried to rise above it for the sake of his family. But inside, he was breaking. Lost. Almost gone.

And then his grandfather came through and filled the room with a beam like sunlight through clouds. Gentle, but powerful. He used my hands to pour love into this man's broken body. Love that didn't come from this world. I felt it rush through me. I couldn't hold back the tears. Then, the message came. Not just of love, but of direction. Precise guidance, specific bank accounts, real estate moves, addresses whispered as if I was reading from a map.

And only then, when his soul was ready, was I allowed to share the vision.

It wasn't an easy one. His future was grim. That was just the way it was designed. But because of free will, he was given two choices. Two doors. Two possible lives. One would keep him locked in the same loop of heartbreak, until his light dimmed for good.

The other, though difficult, would lead him back to himself. To freedom.

I only hope he chose wisely.

LOBSTER

*Abundance

-Plenty and Bounty

-Balance between the exteriors we show the world and our hearts

Clairgustance   L or R

** Time to let go of things that no longer serve you and hold you back like toxic people and negative situations.

-Water = emotions

*Psychic (Great insight movement, restoration and cleansing)

-Put yourself out there.

+ Sexual expression

-Emotional reactions – need aura cleanse

→ Beware – You feel like the dream is slipping away.

-It is time to come out of your shell and allow yourself to be a little more vulnerable

-Walls are keeping life experiences away.

*Know that the universe is giving you a gift even if you perceive it as painful.

*Closed off (love)

-Get a new Hobby

BLOCKS AND CLEANSE

Sacral Chakra – for emotions

EAT: orange foods

CHANT: VAM VAM

DO: Yoga/ warrior and goddess pose

What spirit animal told me my client was suffering from: Menstrual, urinary, lower back pain, sexual imbalance, fatigue

THE LADY FROM ANOTHER REALM

Let me tell you about one of the strange*t* readings I've ever had... and believe me, I've seen some things. It started off as a regular online session with a woman I had never met. Midway through the reading, I felt a shift, a presence appeared to my right. It was like a woman, but not exactly. She was very short, blunt, and honestly, kind of ugly, with this dominant energy that immediately made herself known. She looked me dead in the soul and said:

"Watch yourself. This woman is better than you." Now, I know my role. I'm a messenger, not the center of the message. My job is to put the puzzle together and pass it on. So I kept my cool and described this entity to my client. Her jaw dropped.

She said:

"Omg... it couldn't possibly be?" That's when the entity told me:

"I am not human. I have never been."

And without missing a beat, my client told me the same thing.
They knew each other.
They communicated on another realm.
And then my client said, "Her name is Irma."
That's when the entity told me: "She knows me as Irma."

When I passed that on, my client nearly jumped through the screen with joy. She had been feeling lost and confused about her ability to connect with non-human entities. This moment confirmed everything for her. Then the Holy Spirit came through with a comforting reminder: We see only a small sliver of reality on this planet.

I share this to say: not everything that visits us will look or feel familiar. But that doesn't make it wrong or bad.

I am always protected. I work only with light, with God's grace. And I trust that if something unusual comes through, it's for a reason especially if it brings peace to someone seeking answers.

ELEPHANT

-Remember to look after yourself before helping others.

• You have instincts that will lead you when you need to go.

•Family – including past and future generations

-Shift focus to view whole picture

•Memories

-Young -not all bound by blood

*Connectedness – LOST - Intimacy - HOME

•Meditation

Transformation

*Career

-Clouds

-Beware- you may be influenced by patterns, beliefs, or experiences passed down through family lineage.

! Trauma passed down genetically.

THE ELEPHANT'S GUIDANCE

When the spirit animal elephant came through, I could feel that its presence was powerful and purposeful. I trusted it, as I always do. That day, a woman came to me via online session searching for her mother, who had disappeared without a trace years ago. Her heart carried the weight of every unanswered question.

As I opened myself to Holy Spirit and the energies around her, I was shown a vision. Her mother had passed, her body hidden not by malice, but by nature itself. She had wandered into a wooded area near her home, confused, lost and never returned. Seasons passed. The earth slowly embraced her. But the most important message came next, her neighbors were not to blame, like her children thought.

Her spirit wanted peace for her daughter, not more questions or suspicions. She revealed that she suffered from dementia, and it was that confusion, not foul play, that led her into the forest. When I shared this, my client broke down, confirming that her mother had indeed been diagnosed but vanished before they could help her.

The elephant stood beside us in that moment, a symbol of deep memory, ancestral wisdom, and unwavering truth. It reminded me that some answers come gently, and that even the heaviest truths can bring healing. Through this spirit animal's guidance, my client received not just an ending, but peace.

SWALLOW 12-18 yrs

*Fertility (Womb or business)

-Emotional cleanse

-Seek sympathetic friends and social occasions-do not hide away - it will only make you feel worse

-Reconnection-partner- through proper communication will bring you peace

-Know that you will find success in your profession.

*Watch that you do not sacrifice yourself for people in need.

– Release yourself from expectations.

-Home

*Let go of past hurts and put negative experiences past you!

- Keep an abundance mindset - be more optimistic

BLOCKS AND CLEANSE

Solar Plexus Chakra

WEAR: yellow clothes

DO: Exercise and Aromatherapy

CHANT: RAAAM

What spirit animal told me my client was suffering from: Tiered, anger, father issues, anxiety trauma, poor digestion, gas, nausea, diabetes, respiratory issues, arthritis, abdominal pain, nerve pain

A JOURNEY OF HEALING AND REBIRTH

I had a client who came to me simply saying she wasn't feeling well. Nothing more, just an overwhelming sense of being off. As I listened, I felt the presence of her grandfather strong, protective, and loving. But then, something deeper and more emotional emerged. Her father came through as well, and with him, an energy of remorse, sadness, and regret. He was there to apologize for the way she had been raised, for the trauma she and her mother had endured at his hands. What followed was a revelation. I was shown that from the age of twelve, my client had been suffering with extreme anxiety, so much so that it led her to believe the world had no place for her. Her emotional and physical well-being began to deteriorate. Suicidal thoughts plagued her teenage years. Around the age of eighteen, she started attracting relationships with men who mirrored the very toxicity she had grown up with. These relationships were abusive, leaving deep scars that were carried into her adult life. Spirit then guided me to take her through a hypnosis session, she met with her father in a sacred space to accept his apology. The weight of years of emotional baggage began to lift. Together, we also worked on healing her body, which had been carrying not only physical trauma but emotional wounds that had been suppressed for far too long. I blessed her womb with herbs, water, myrrh, and dried flowers, sending intentions of fertility, rebirth, and empowerment. I could feel the shift in her energy as the cleanse began to take hold. I hope that in the days following, she was able to feel a renewed sense of peace and clarity. The swallow had come to show her that healing is a process that sometimes requires confronting old wounds, accepting apologies that are long overdue, and, most importantly, allowing yourself to let go.

HORNET

30-36 years
-Unexpected change
-Tiered of being held back
-Disagreements- guests who have nothing good in mind
-Difficult communicating - words come harshly and have distinct sting, be careful who you direct it at
*Organize your space - free of clutter
*Make a plan, remember greatness takes time.
> What is in your way? Look around at every angle-
*Brocken Heart! -hard to open up - afraid of intimacy
*Deep emotional Cleanse

PRAY FOR: foundation, development, fertility (womb or business), breakthroughs and advancements, productivity, articulation, honesty with self and others

BLOCKS AND CLEANSE
Third Eye Chakra
WEAR: Indigo Colors and Amathyst crystals
EAT: Figs, grapes, prunes, eggplant, cabbage,
TAKE: Melatonin
PRACTICE Visualization

What spirit animal told me my client was suffering from:
Winter blues, repeated pattern

THE STING BEFORE THE SOOTHING

Some readings don't begin with peace and ease, they begin with chaos. A few hours before my online session, I felt it hit me. My thoughts were bouncing uncontrollably. I was hyper, scattered, and overwhelmed. At this point in my path, I know that if my next client suffers from something, I will feel it before the reading. So, I knew exactly what it meant: I was feeling my client's nerves and tension.

When the session began, everything around her seemed to reflect her inner world. She was distracted, annoyed by a random noise in her home, and couldn't get her speakers to work right. But I stayed grounded, inhaled deeply, and called in the energy of love. That's when a deep sense of empathy filled my lungs.

She was heartbroken, freshly separated from a long-term relationship. And worse, she felt abandoned by her family for being gay. Working from home had intensified her ADHD and OCD, and she described her days as feeling like the walls were closing in.

Through her spirit animal message, I was shown what needed to be said. Not from judgment, but from understanding. She needed divine answers, not sugar-coated ones but strong, clear truth delivered with gentleness.

As I passed on the messages, I saw her begin to soften, even behind the screen. The chaos she carried had a source, but it also had a solution.

And even though I haven't seen her since, I pray she's in a better place now calmer, more centered, and beginning to understand that sometimes, the sting comes first... but healing always follows.

CATERPILLAR

*Change
-Going through a difficult change in life, know that you will evolve with grace in your own time
-Expect fresh ideas, renewal and unexpected, outcomes
-Be patient even if things don't look good
*Elegant metamorphosis
- Remember some things appear delectable but are not good for you.
*Fine tune your intuition!!!
*Everything will come in its due season.
-Remember there is so much more in the world that you must experience with more than your 5 senses. Open yourself to energies, see with other eyes.
→ Surprise is coming for you -financial promotion
-Beware of those who lie and bring false hope- listen to when your hair stands up-take step back and don't rush into decisions especially in business -let things evolve
! Break out of your shell and embrace your personal and spiritual inheritance as a child of the universe.
-Practice humility and meekness
-Beware or repeating cycles

BLOCKS AND CLEANSE
Sacral Chakra
WEAR: Orange
EAT: Orange foods
HEAL IN: Water
CHANT: VAM
BE IN: Inspirational environments

PRACTICE: Yoga and reflexology below the wrists and the sole of the feet

What spirit animal told me my client was suffering from: Emotional blockages, lack of creativity, lack of sexual energy, abusive mom, codependency

BABY BOY
She came to me with quiet eyes and a heart full of hope wanting a child, but feeling time was running out. What she didn't expect was that the first one to arrive was a child. Her partner's baby boy who had passed came through with such a soft strength. His energy was gentle, playful, and full of love. He helped me deliver her spirit animal message with a clarity that felt sacred. He passed on messages for his father urging him to return to the joy of soccer, and to live a little more. But most of all, he gave this woman hope. He reminded her that miracles don't check our age or status. They check our hearts.

There are times, after a reading, that I thank God for keeping me tuned in, fully, deeply, and with no judgment. Because the message I was given to deliver wasn't about logic, it was about faith. She had been through so much.

A controlling mother, emotional wounds, deep-rooted blockages... and yet, she still believed in love, in healing, and in the possibility of new life. And so, I said what Spirit gave me. No filters. No doubts. Just love.

"You still have time." You still have hope." I walked away from that session with love and gratitude in my heart. I felt so grateful that I didn't let disbelief interrupt a divine message. I pray her wish came true. I pray she's holding something small and sacred today. And I hope she knows that she was never too late.

SWAN

-Under pressure?

-Troubling romance (loss)

- It is time to examine how you are moving through the world.

-Grow in your intuitive nature, open yourself to the energies all around you so that you can see and know differently.

-Pay attention to your instincts and honor them.

-Death and rebirth-

self-esteem inner grace and beauty

-You must embrace all of you.

-You are a natural healer and seer.

-Sing!

-Find your voice and carry your own.

-Learn new ways of thinking, breathing, and going with the flow of life

PRAY FOR: Spirituality, harmony, love

BLOCK AND CLEANSE
Throat Chakra
Solar Plexus Chakra

THE SWAN'S MESSAGE

Some moments in my work leave me in complete awe, reminding me why I always trust in spirit animals. This was one of them. The day before my readings, a swan appeared to me on my gratitude walk. I felt it immediately; this was my sign. What I didn't know was that it would be for three different clients.

In my first session, the swan guided me into a deep mediumship reading for a mother who had lost her daughter to suicide. It had only been a short time since her passing, so I didn't expect it, yet her daughter came through so clearly. I knew why. Her mother's love transcended all pain, all judgment, all guilt. She understood the soul's journey, and because of that, her daughter was able to reach her without resistance.

She shared specifics about her passing, moments only her mother would know. And then she mentioned her blue purse a small but undeniable validation that her spirit was truly there. It was one of the most beautiful connections I had ever witnessed. Her mother was a testament to unconditional love, a rare kind that allows souls to reunite without barriers.

Later that day, after my meditation, I heard the Holy Spirit whisper: "Use the same spirit animal message. This time, it was for a mother who had lost her son to an accidental overdose. Just like before, her child was able to come through, not in pain, not in regret, but in love. Because his mother held no anger, no shame, only the need to tell him she loved him, one more time. And he heard her. He explained his reasons, gave her understanding, and I only hope it brought her peace.

The next morning, during prayer, I heard the Holy Spirit whisper: "Use the same spirit animal message."

I didn't question it. I never do.

During my session, the swan's message returned once more, guiding a woman who questioned her future as a wife and mother. But this time, something was different.

There were hidden truths within her heart, things she had kept herself. As spirit revealed her path, I felt an overwhelming sense of tenderness, of gentleness, of pure understanding. Spirit did not judge her. It did not condemn her. It only held space for her truth. She had been carrying the weight of an affair, wrestling with the emotions it stirred, guilt, longing, confusion. But here, in this space, spirit spoke only in love. The swan guided her to follow her heart, to release the shame, and to see herself through the eyes of compassion. I was deeply moved. In the spiritual realm, only love exists. There is no punishment, no ridicule, no labels of "right" or "wrong "only the purest understanding of who we are and what we need to learn. She left not just with answers, but with something far greater, forgiveness and love for herself and her own journey. But the swan's work wasn't done. During each of their sessions, the swan showed me where all three of my clients share the same blocks deep within their throat Chakra and solar plexus. Their voices, their personal power, their ability to fully step into their truth held back by the unseen weight of their individual loss and confusion.

So, I performed a spiritual limpia (cleanse)

Through energy work, I cleared these blocks, allowing harmony to return. And more than that, I set an intention guided by the swan for their spirituality, their love, their inner peace to expand.

The swan reminded me that spirit always shows up at the right time, with the right message, for the right person.

HORSE

-Trapped feeling like you want to explode
-Reclaim your personal power
-Put down things you no longer need!
-Time to choose a new path forward
* Use the power of air to cleanse your aura
-Relax, enjoy what you have – travel - take a trip
-Remember you have the power to change everything
you choose in your life.
*Remember your journey as a whole.
-share your gifts- this will give you power

PRAY FOR: Inspiration and creativity

BLOCKS AND CLEANSE
Sacral Chakra

THE HORSE'S PATH

She came to me asking for a prayer to clear her mind.
Didn't say much. But 99% of the time, I feel my clients
before they even speak, and this time was no different.
The moment I laid my hands on her, I felt it her silent
desperation to get pregnant.
Spirit filled in the rest. She felt stuck, overwhelmed, like
she was carrying a weight too big for her body. Spirit
showed me the path ahead. It wouldn't be easy. Her
stomach would need to go through the process, IVF,
injections, and emotions she hadn't even touched yet. I
could feel she didn't want to hear that. But I also saw a
light. There was still hope.
Then I was guided by angels who led me to do a water
limpia (water cleanse) for her. I used herbs, dried

flowers, and teas I brought back from Petra, Jordan. I used fresh mint and parsley to splash her with the sacred water. Then, I softly scratched her belly with a dried sea horse I got in Thailand. She stayed still the whole time, eyes closed. I think she felt something lift. I sent the remaining water with her in a jar for her to bathe in. I just hope that whatever spirit showed me that day finds her.

WHITE PEACOCK

-You have the ability to see and understand with the eye of the heart.

-Nothing including beauty should be taken too seriously.

-Take everything lightly, don't let things bother you!

-Remember laughter is the best medicine to stay healthy happy.

*It is time to acknowledge your dreams and aspirations.

*Find your way back to gratitude.

*Know that confidence, stature, and accomplishment in everything you do surround you.

*They are here to help make life not feel dull and drab.

-Color / Renewal / Support

•Medicine = move, work

• Smudge your home with sage and peacock feathers.

*Don't give up on your dreams.

*Improve your relationship with your sacred masculine.

•Step into your power.

1.Identify limiting beliefs or wounds you may carry around masculine energy.

2.Self-discipline -set clear goals

3.Stand up for yourself.

4.Self-confidence.

5. Balance your intuition and emotions.

• Personal growth.

- wellness

-sidelines

• Practice Letting go!

BLOCKS AND CLEANSE

•Solar plexus – confidence and will power

•Sacral Chakra -creativity, passion, balance feminine and masculine energies, goals
•Root Chakra -safety, stability grounded
DO: Breathwork
BATHE: Lavendar
WEAR: Amulet

THE MESSENGER IN WHITE: A TALE OF TWO PATHS
Early that morning, during prayer, I heard again, Holy Spirit guiding me to two sessions with messages that would come from the same spirit animal. To make it even clearer, on my gratitude walk, I was shown a vision of two male energies. I didn't know who they were yet, but I knew their messages were coming.
Later that day, in my online session, the two male energies from my vision appeared, not in spirit, but as representation of two brothers, one being my client. Instead, it was their father who came through in spirit through a mediumship reading. He was seeking forgiveness from his son, my client. After, he gave him a firm but loving message. "Leave your brother alone. Let him fight his own battles and walk his own path." In the end it was a message of release, of stepping back, of allowing destiny to unfold without interference. Then, in my in-person session, the two male energies I had seen were both deceased. One was my client's father, the other, her husband's baby brother. Her father stepped forward, bringing guidance about business and finances, urging her to trust, to take action, and to receive the help available to her from the spirit world. In both sessions, the white peacock revealed the same energetic blocks, imbalances in the sacral, solar

plexus, and root Chakras. Blocks that kept them stuck, struggling, unable to move forward fully. With this awareness, I was able to help clear and realign their energy, bringing a sense of balance and harmony back into their path.

The white peacock showed me once again, spirit knows exactly what needs to be healed and who is ready to receive it.

EAGLE

-You are blessed with messages from other realms but need help on what to make of them
*Renewal, great change is headed your way
-Stand up tall, be brave, and stay true to yourself.
*Make time for wellness
-Sometimes you need to be forceful.
-Be very sure of your movements

PRAY FOR: Streght, courage, resistance, job, relationship

BLOCKS AND CLEANSE
Third Eye Chakra and Throat Chakra
DO: sing
CHANT: OM and HAM
EAT: Blue diet
WEAR: blue crystal in pocket
DRINK: peppermint, sage, and thyme teas

What spirit animal told me my client was suffering from: confusion, lack of clarity, constant over thinking, headaches, eyestrain, blurred vision, sinus, fear, anxiety

THE HEART OF AN UNWANTED SON

He came out of curiosity. A man with strong presence, his words filled the room before I could even speak. I let him lead. Sometimes that's how healing begins. I let the silence stretch just enough to soften him, while I opened the door quietly and stepped into his heart. With Holy Spirit as my guide, I began reading his soul. I walked the path of his life, from the first memories of his boyhood to the man sitting in front of me that day. And I saw it, the ache no one had dared name. A lifetime shaped by a father whose love had never fully arrived. A man who had learned to be loud so he wouldn't be ignored.

His spirit animal, the Eagle, had come through days before. Bold and powerful, meant to soar, but wounded at the wing. I spoke his secrets softly but clearly. Not to break him, but to remind him that they no longer had to break him. The burden he carried wasn't his to hold anymore. When I spoke of his father's indifference, I saw the melt happen. It wasn't dramatic. It was quiet. Heavy. Real.

We spoke about dominance, control, and how to untie the invisible knots that bind. Spirit gave him tools. A way forward. Wellness, clarity, strength. A call to rise, not in defense, but in freedom.

Before he left, I prayed he would find peace in the soul cluster he belongs to. So that he may rest when this lifetime is done. I carry him in prayer. I pray one day he finds the love he craves.

DUCK
• Take notice - new opportunities are available to you
• Take action now on current project
emotions
→ Path of self-discovery, spirituality, freedom, and higher consciousness
! Go for it !
-Interaction and community-needed
- Speak up-share your vision
        ->People do not know what they want unless you speak up.
*Relationship - be patient don't over analyze - red flags?
-Remember laughter brings joy and is a powerful healer.
• Remember selfcare includes spiritual nurturing - protect your sacred self!
•Don't keep extending yourself to those who don't give back.

<u>BLOCKS AND CLEANSE</u>
Third eye Chakra- others are taking advantage of you
Throat Chakra – speak up
Sacral Chakra for emotions
Root Chakra – grounding and survival

THE ALLEY
One morning in Prague, I was walking through one of its narrow, hidden alleyways. The kind only the locals know. Quiet, old, full of stories. That's when the spirit of the duck came to me.
Later that day, a woman came in for a session. It had been gifted to her. She was sweet, polite, and soft. But she wasn't seeking anything. She didn't want answers.

She wasn't curious or even slightly intrigued. She was just... there.

As I laid my hands over her and began to pray, I could feel it, her soul was out of balance. Not in chaos, just distant. She was carrying something she couldn't name.

Spirit told me clearly: "Watch your tongue."

I was only allowed to share what flowed, a simple, vague, unassuming message. Nothing deep, nothing powerful. So, I honored that.

But the moment I prayed, I felt Holy Spirit pour through me. Not in words, but in love. Pure, quiet, unconditional love. It wrapped around her like warm water.

When she left, I stayed behind to cleanse the space. And that's when I heard it clearly in my spirit:

"Veronica, you can't expect those who aren't looking for answers to find them. And those who don't know they lack... to seek."

That brought me peace.

FLEA

-You are obtaining energy from others, especially those closest to you, even without realizing it

*Beware of physical, emotional, and other vampirisms.

*Beware of unhealthy reliance on others + others prey upon your energy since you give too much of it away!

! Stay alert for a new opportunity

-Seek quiet, dark places for restoration and refuge

-Take stock of your situation / too much stimulation

*Blood wisdom, secrets, memories connect to your ancestors

-Learn to give and take-

*Energy drain-examine your relationships

BLOCKS AND CLEANSE
Solar plexus Chakra
WEAR: yellow

What spirit animal told me my client was suffering from: Overcontrolling, fear of saying "No", lack of self-esteem, lack of direction and purpose, unresolved emotional patterns, no boundaries, trauma (child)

THE COST OF STAYING

She came to me looking perfectly put together, beautiful, polished, composed. But the moment I opened with prayer; Holy Spirit showed me everything. I was taken into her world, deep and fast. Her relationship was done, over, but still physically alive. He no longer loved her. In fact, he loathed her. Spirit showed me how he stayed, not out of love, but out of lack. He didn't earn enough to survive alone, and she, knowingly or not, had wrapped herself around that truth like armor. She had bought time, not love. She was hoping he'd come back around.

The spirit animal flea had already come to me before our session. I now understood why. It revealed the energy exchange was not love, it was survival, and it was draining them both.

When I spoke, Spirit didn't let me sugarcoat it. I was direct. Firm. But kind. She cried. Not because she was surprised, but because she already knew. She had just needed someone to say it out loud. As tears rolled down her cheeks, Holy Spirit wrapped her in comfort. And another truth came through, one she didn't expect. Spirit warned her of her pattern: finding refuge in friendships she had to buy. People who fed on her kindness and gave little in return.

Then something beautiful happened.

Spirit told her she would move. Far from all of this. In three years, she'd find herself in a different life, with a different man. I told her. She laughed through her tears.

It's in readings like this, where the truth hurts but heals, that I feel the deepest kind of empathy. When someone comes in seeking love, and they walk away knowing it starts within.

DOLPHIN

**Self-love   **Playful Alert

-Heavy emotions

-Remember to navigate relationships while maintaining self-respect

-Diplomat

-Air/water

-You are very protected – family, young, sick

-Entering a period of renewal and rebirth

-Remember when one door closes another opens.

•Reclaim your voice!

*Do a cleanse to help with bad memories and feelings from the past.

*Suffering from trauma of belittlement

-Feeling blocked from your natural playful self

    BLOCKS:
1. Solar Plexus Chakra
2. Heart Chakra
3. Throat Chakra

THE DOLPHIN'S HEALING TOUCH

The dolphin came to me in a vision, playful yet deeply knowing. I didn't yet understand its purpose, but I trusted that soon, I would. During my reading's opening prayer, I placed my hands on a young girl, and instantly, I felt her pain. Not just the ache of a broken heart but the sting that covered her skin. Rosacea. It wasn't just physical; it carried the weight of deep emotional wounds.

Then, it happened. Holy Spirit guided me to my spirit council, the presence of many who take over me, allowing me to channel their divine wisdom and interpret it into a human message easy to understand. The holy ones. I call them Elohim. Their energy surged through me, flowing like a river of light, wrapping around her with love, cleansing, restoring. Through the guidance of the dolphin and the power of the Elohim, healing poured out of my entire being, my aura, my eternal existence and into hers. A cleanse, unlike any other instant, profound, and sacred occurred, although she didn't yet know it, I did and so I cried.

Weeks passed. Then, one day, she found me again. In her hands, a simple note. It simply said: "Veronica, thank you. You helped me cure my allergy. It hasn't occurred since our siting. I feel free and feminine. You are love of the world"

The dolphin had led her to healing. The holy ones had restored her. And once again, I was reminded that when we surrender to Holy Spirit's divine unconditional love, miracles happen.

BUNNY

-Plan - it's time for decision

-Others are taking advantage of you.

-Stop, look, and listen like never before.

• Cornered

* Personal transformation is necessary and about to happen.

-STOP victim mentality "trust your smarts and know that are worthy of respect"

→Thinking of larger family

• Effective family planning is necessary to avoid overextending yourself physically, emotionally, or financially

•It is ok when things move fast as long as you have daily plan.

-FEAR -focusing on whatever frightens you is calling it into your life

PRAY FOR: Job, home, problems within

<u>BLOCKS AND CLEANSE</u>
Root Chakra

What spirit animal told me my client was suffering from: Disconnection, voiceless, stuck, lost, depleted

A MESSAGE FROM AN OLD FRIEND

She came to me for spiritual advice, but before I could even begin, her best friend from elementary school was already standing beside her. I didn't need confirmation. She came with love in her heart and a gentle nudge to say hi to her sister. The three of them had been like a little tribe once two still here on Earth, one now guiding from the spirit realm.

Her presence helped me ease into the reading with tenderness. Spirit animal Bunny had come through earlier with messages that needed careful delivery, gentle, but honest. With her friend helping from the other side, I was able to speak clearly into the pain in her marriage. The love there had changed, and Spirit was showing the cracks that were quietly draining her. She had been feeling cornered, pushing through her days like most women do, carrying her business, her motherhood, her marriage, and her dreams on her back, not realizing how much of herself she'd been giving away. We talked about her business, her home life, and her hope for another child. Spirit guided her to pause. To make a real plan. Not from fear but from her own worth. Her energy was leaking in places she didn't see. She'd been trying to do it all without asking for enough support.

We cleared the root Chakra that day. Her friend stood close the whole time, steady, smiling, proud. I know she heard me when I prayed for her afterward.

I'm always in awe of women like her. Holding so many roles, wearing so many faces, and still showing up with grace.

TURTLE

•Patience, perseverance, wisdom, grounding
-Trust the timing, process of your life
-Stay centered no matter where you are.
-Slow down – you seek validation when you are crazy busy.
-Stay true to yourself.
*Work = change
-> water - water - water! = baths, play, travel
*Earthly body-take good care of it!
-Take your time before you move.
-Use your own head, you are powerful enough to better yourself, even when others don't believe you can.
-A spiritual guardian is with you to bless you with a long life.
• Remember when your world seems shaky, it is Great Spirit shaking you - meaning its time make adjustments.
#13
-Full moon
*Emotions / fertility
✓ protection – love and peace
-Your constant worry comes from a past life no need to worry now, you are blessed here with great luck.

PRAY FOR: Loneliness, broken heart, Insecurity, Inability to receive Love

BLOCKS AND CLEANSE
1.Root Chakra 2. Heart Chakra

THE TURTLE'S GUIDANCE

Sometimes, spirit has other plans. I had a reading scheduled, but just before, I was told to cancel it. No explanation just a deep knowing that I needed to listen. So, I did.

Instead, I went on my gratitude walk through the old town, letting spirit guide my steps. That's when I found myself drawn to a hidden space an old sunken room now transformed into a coffee shop and vintage store. It sat beside an ancient church, holding the energy of countless stories from the past. As I stepped inside, I was met with an unexpected vision, a grandfather, standing in the quiet corners of the space. He wasn't there in body, but in spirit. He showed me something specific, a delicate tea set, placed with care as if waiting to be remembered.

The next day, I understood why. In my reading, the same grandfather came through, this time with a message of love and hope for his granddaughter, a woman he had never met in life. She had come to me seeking answers, guidance for the path ahead. But before she could trust the message, he made sure she knew it was truly him. He spoke her son's name, a detail only family could have known. That was all it took, her heart opened, and she listened.

The turtle spirit had brought me patience, reminding me that sometimes, messages unfold in their own time. And in that quiet, steady way, it led a grandfather's love exactly where it needed to go.

LADY BUG

-Feeling underestimated   #16
-Looking for a little more love in your life
*Inner child work
- Goals will begin to manifest in a remarkable way
-Don't worry or be scared. Live and honor yourself.
*Relationship ->love
#You will be stepping into a role of helper / healer.
-You will make a difference in the life of others, this will help you evolve.
-You are so much fun don't forget that about yourself.

PRAY FOR: wholeness, safety, dignity, love, spiritual exploration, fertility of business

BLOCKS AND CLEANSE
Sacral Chakra
WEAR: orange
DO: yoga / warrior goddess pose

What spirit animal told me my client was suffering from: menstrual, urinary, sexual interests, back pain, closed off, uncomfortable, body insecurities, lost

A WHISPER TOWARD HER DESTINY
On one of my morning gratitude walks, a small but powerful spirit landed right on my hand, a ladybug. She stayed with me just long enough to say *"16."* (She was born on the 16th day of the month).
That afternoon, I had an online session with a young woman who had a session with me the previous year. She was sweet, quiet, with eyes that held more than words ever could.

She had returned, this time looking for direction. When I connected to her energy, it felt soft and pure. I melted into the love frequency that surrounded her. I knew someone would come through; I had seen him in my vision earlier on my gratitude walk. Then, her grandfather came forward, gentle and wise, and stood behind her with a steady hand on her shoulder. He nudged her gently toward change.

He wanted her to return to her roots, to go back to the European Union, to find herself again in the familiar land where her spirit could expand. He reminded her how much life there is waiting for her, if she dares to bloom. The ladybug spirit whispered: "You're not lost. You're underestimated even by yourself."

This reading reminded me how important it is for young women to be told:

You are enough.

You are beautiful. You are powerful. And you are meant to evolve into a helper, a healer, someone who will one day light the path for others. It was such a soft, magical moment. I'm always so humbled when clients return it means Spirit has touched something in them that keeps growing.

FLAMINGO

①- Balance in your life

-Time to stand strong in the face of changes

-West Indies / Galapagos /Africa / Midde East / Andes Mountains

->Florida

· Giraffes, Gorillas

-Time to introduce yoga into your life-

-Pink color-playful charming personality resonates with harmony -openness

*Create community ties you can trust.

-They have seen you count your blessings and being a champion for keeping the faith.

· Keep an eye on your emotions

• If you are spending way too much time on tasks instead of living joyfully, pause and give back to yourself. Find what makes you happy and do it. It is true that everyone has responsibilities – but those necessities are not 24/7.

-Find pauses, the quiet space where potential waits, catch your potential, your breath. Even if only for a few minutes. Here and there, it makes a difference.

-Pause socially – between words, let things sink in.

-Pause before making life changing decisions.

-Yellow traffic light

-Your beauty is far more than skin deep.

-Pay attention to your new love interests.

-Remember that you can seek guidance when you feel you have "2 left feet".

*Ask yourself - I'm I trying to reach? Ensure your steps are first possible, within reason.

•You are a heart healer with psychic insight and highly flirtatious, you embody beauty and spiritual lightness- use it, own it, spread it!
Unresolved emotions

BLOCKS AND CLEANSE
Root Chakra
WEAR: red clothes, crystals – red jasper, red garnet
EAT: red foods
REPEAT "I am safe, I am grounded, I am supported" affirmations

What spirit animal told me my client was suffering from: Unbalanced energy at the base of spine, insecurity, fear, instability, financial struggles, anxiety, lack of motivation, lower back pain, fatigue, digestion

BALANCED IN GRACE
During my meditation, a vivid pink flamingo appeared so graceful, balanced, and standing tall. I knew immediately that it carried a message for my next client. She was an artist at a crossroads, transitioning into a new form of creative expression. She sought clarity on her direction, unsure if she was making the right move. As we began the session, spirit opened the door for her loved ones to step forward. Her grandmother, father, aunt, and cousin all came through with messages of reassurance and encouragement. They reminded her that she was on the right path, that her gifts were evolving as they were meant to, and that fear should not hold her back.
Holy Spirit led me to perform a deep cleanse for her, specifically focusing on her feet. She had been feeling

ungrounded, uncertain, and weighed down by doubt. The cleansing lifted the heaviness, allowing her to feel lighter, more connected, and ready to step forward in confidence.

By the end of the session, the flamingo's message was clear. It was time for her to find balance, trust, and faith in her own journey. Her loved ones had shown up not just to guide her, but to remind her that she was never walking this path alone.

HIPPO

-Hiding from feelings
-Needs emotional foundation healing
*Potential for greatness if you pursue and seek spiritual knowledge
-Goals and ideas
-Speak your mind
Water Use water to heal your emotions
*Remember things are not always as the seem and your eyes can deceive you.
-Teeth (check)
-Face the situation you've been avoiding and stand strong in your convictions.
- Stagnant-
-Oversensitive –
-Be careful that you don't see problems where there may not be any.
-Toughen up so chaos doesn't wipe you out on an emotional or energetic level.
-Artistic expression
-Honest communication
-You need to share your story, express your ideas, "Shout it from the rooftops"

BLOCKS AND CLEANSE
Root Chakra
WEAR: red clothes, crystals – red jasper
EAT: red foods
REPEAT "I am supported" affirmations
DO: Implement visualization techniques
TAKE: baths to cleanse stagnant energy
PRACTICE: healthy boundaries

THE VOICE BENEATH THE SURFACE

She came to me quiet, distant, closed off in a way I see far too often. Her energy sat heavy, like it had been held underwater too long. When I tuned into her field, I could feel how deep the pain went especially from the women in her family. Her beauty had never been celebrated. I hugged her and loved her. I honored her because I could feel that her voice had been silenced before it ever had the chance to speak its truth.

Spirit showed me the emotional bruises mostly from her mother and sister and how much she had internalized their rejection.
Spirit said: "She's not just holding back... she's hiding."

And so, I took her hands in mine. I stared at them; I smelled them, and I could smell that she was hiding from her feelings.
She wanted answers to questions she didn't have. She was afraid to express what she couldn't name. Her gifts, spiritual, intuitive, creative, were trapped behind walls built by survival.

We spoke about her power, her purpose, and her role as a mother. Spirit urged to share her the truth, her story, her healing with others. I saw that one day, she would become a voice that helps others rise on a stage, behind a mic, in a room full of women like her.

I did an egg cleanse, asking Spirit to pull the trapped energy from her body. There was so much hidden within her. So much potential stuck in still water.
I prayed for her emotional foundation because it would need healing before the world could witness her greatness.

Even now, I wish I could've done more...
But I also know this: Healing doesn't happen all at once.
And sometimes, the deepest transformation begins with one person holding space for what someone can't yet say.
I pray she remembers who she is and on the days she can't, I hope she feels my love.
And I pray one day, we'll hear her shout it from the rooftops.

SANDPIPER

-Find peace in the in-between you are not lost, you are transitioning.
-Embrace solitude without loneliness; clarity often arrives when you walk alone.
-Stay light on your feet don't carry what isn't yours.
-Emotions come in waves, ride them with grace, don't resist.
-Observe more, react less. Your sensitivity is a gift, not a burden.
-Keep your heart open, even when the world feels too loud.
-You don't need to shout to be heard your quiet presence is powerful.
-Trust the timing of your path
-Seek joy in simple things.
-Inner work – renew your thoughts and beliefs
-Protect your peace
Cleanse your energy with wind and water
-ego-
*Shadow work

PRAY FOR: Emotional clarity, grace in transitions, Inner peace

BLOCKS AND CLEANSE
Heart and throat Chakra
WEAR: soft blues, seafoam green
DO: walk near water, journal
DRINK: peppermint, blue lotus, lemon balm
CHANT: "VAM" (to balance sensitivity with flow)

HER HOLY ACT

She came to see me because she believed. You could tell. The way she spoke, the way she sat across from me. I think she hoped her mom would come through. She had just passed, and I know that kind of grief. The kind where all you want is a sign, a whisper, anything that says your person still exists.

But right in the middle of the session, someone else stepped in. Not expected, not even particularly welcomed. His presence was sharp and awkward, like a memory you'd rather not visit. Her father-in-law, stern in life, proud in posture now appeared with his head bowed low, not in shame, but in recognition.

His soul didn't come cloaked in charm or poetic words. He was rough, rigid, and real, as she remembered. But in death, he found humility.

He didn't ask for forgiveness outright. But he showed her how he had watched her, how, despite everything, she honored him when he no longer had breath. He spoke of his hands, how honored his body. Her act was holy. He knew that now. He thanked her in the only way he knew how, and then he left swift, like a gust of wind that moves the trees and disappears.

She sat in silence and a sense of validation. Her pain had been witnessed by Spirit. Her love had been acknowledged. I laid her down on my treatment table and began the cleanse with light hands, prayerful breath, feathers, palo santo and water.

I swept away what didn't belong to her. Because I know that grief can cling like mist.

After she left, I stayed behind and thanked God for her. For her vulnerability, her strength. For her willingness to sit with the pain and still search for love.

She is my sister, my friend. And every night, I ask Holy Spirit to let her mother come back through me one day, just for a chat, just to say one more thing, crack a joke, or remind her of that one time.

That is my prayer.

WOLF

-Unconditional love
-Support leading your pack at work or home
-Bark or bite
-Know that you are protected.
-Its ok to have fun once in a while.
• Destruction and dissolution -> protection and healing

PRAY FOR: Adaptibility

<u>BLOCKS AND CLEANSE</u>
Solar Plexus Chakra
WEAR: yellow clothing
DO: walk in the sun, meditate
DRINK: ginger, turmeric
CHANT: RAM

What spirit animal told me my client was suffering from:
Head trauma, depression, sadness, lack of energy,
anger, frustration, low self-esteem, anxiety, stomach

GO TO THE MISSION

During my prayer I was immediately pulled into a vision.
Somewhere between Arizona and New Mexico, where
the red earth breathes, and the wind still carries ancient
voices. Later that morning I had an online session. A
woman appeared on my screen, and even before she
spoke, I could feel the call of our ancestors. I knew then
and there that she hadn't come to me by coincidence.
Our Native blood, rooted deep and sacred, had
summoned her for something more than just a reading.
She was on a mission that perhaps even she didn't fully
understand yet.

As we began, Spirit opened doors quickly and without hesitation. I was shown flashes of her body, her home, and her family's business. Everything was connected the tension at home, the choices waiting to be made, the things unsaid between relatives. Through remote viewing, I was allowed to view not just her present life, but the direction she was heading in, the decisions she had not yet made, and the effects those decisions would have if left unchecked. Sometimes Spirit gives me a glimpse, and sometimes it gives me a clear road, and for her, it was the road.

The stress was lingering heavily around her, like smoke that wouldn't clear. The pressure of the family dynamic was not just emotional, it had begun to show up in her physical health. For some people, these weights go unnoticed until the body begins to speak through pain, fatigue, or unexplained sickness. I told her what I saw, gently, not to frighten her but to offer her the truth.

It was then that her elders came through. I could feel them gather around me with quiet strength. They helped me perform a spiritual cleanse over her body, not just for what had already begun to affect her physically, but to protect her from the things that were still forming, the heaviness of thoughts, resentment, fear, and expectations that do not belong to her spirit. She came to me needing clarity, but I believe what she really received was the strength to carry her mission forward. And I pray she does.

MOOSE

- Family -

*Water

-Difficult situation

-Don't be concerned about what those around on may think.

-You have to live for yourself, your vision, and your purpose.

-Don't give into outside pressure when you know that the advice is wrong.

smell *eyesight*

-Take better care of yourself regarding your diet. Get professional advice regarding nutrients.

*Sensitive feelings

! You are here for a reason

*Remember that you and only you have the authority to make choices in your life.

*Do not let yourself be pressured by friends and peers.

-Stand loud and proud of who you are.

PRAY FOR: self-esteem, identity, decision making, courage, ambition

BLOCKS AND CLEANSE
Solar Plexus Chakra
WEAR: yellow clothes
DRINK: Chamomile and ginger teas
DO: Dance

What spirit animal told me my client was suffering from: Controlling, dominating, angry, arrogance

LOUD AND PROUD

She was young and had a beautiful face. She must have been around twenty-two, maybe twenty-three. Spirit showed me a wall around her heart so high, even her own light couldn't get in. She came seeking "direction," or so she said, but the moment I placed my hands over her to pray, I knew that didn't believe. Not in Spirit. Not in the reading. And definitely not in spirit animals.

She believed only in herself. Sometimes I wonder why souls like hers even find their way to my doorstep. But then I remember: not every exchange is for them. Some are for me to stay strong in my faith.
To keep showing up with love, even in disbelief. The moose came forward before our session began. Stubborn, proud and guarded. When I closed my eyes, Spirit made it clear that this young woman was being pulled in all the wrong directions by friends who had no business directing her life.
I delivered the message with kindness but firmness: "You must live for yourself. For your purpose. Your calling. Not theirs. "But with every word, her eyes grew more distant and skeptical.

So, I stopped speaking to her mind and began speaking to her heart. I connected to God.

To the Source of all truth. And I asked Spirit to let the message pass through the judgment she wore like armor.

I performed a cleanse, releasing the sticky energy of doubt and arrogance from her field. I asked the angels to take it, recycle it and to turn her disbelief into something the Earth could work with. To return it as love. Maybe one day, her Moose message will click. Maybe one day, she'll feel the truth of what was said. Maybe not. For me, it doesn't matter. I don't need to understand it all. Because even when they doubt, I don't. Not in Spirit. Not in God. And not in the sacred work I was put here to do.

And maybe... just maybe... this was for me.

To stand loud and proud, like the moose...no matter who's listening.

OPPOSUM

-Help strategizing
-Feeling misunderstood and underestimated
Come back to life
* Instead of fighting, come up with a more peaceful approach
*Blind / hidden truths
->highly protected spirit
*Adventure travel
*New endeavors
OPTIONS when considering examine if you have all the support, you need before diving in
Or do they
      - take you away from cherished goals
      -leave you exposed and vulnerable
-Look hard at the persons and situations in your life - walk away to keep your mind, body, and spirit safe
*Focus on your psychic abilities and senses - with this you will awaken talent and abilities from past lives
-Do work on your inner child
-Remember you are a survivor.
-Be patient.

PRAY FOR: stability, practicality, focus, strength

BLOCKS AND CLEANSE
Third eye Chakra
-WEAR: Purple clothes, crystals
-EAT: purple diet, fresh seeds and nuts, rosemary, sage, and thyme
-DO: yoga stretches, journal / keep a diary

What spirit animal told me my client was suffering from: Eye strain, headaches, difficulty concentrating, feeling disconnected, tension in the brow area, sinus problems, dizziness, self-doubt, problems with skin

RAINBOW CONTRACT

They arrived in a whirlwind of panic and unraveling threads. The father had come to me before, but this time was different. He was soaked in sweat, his face red and distressed. His words fell out in frantic bursts, too fast to hold but heavy enough to weigh down the room: "I don't know what to do. I feel like giving up. My son, please help him. He's out of control. Please, you're our last hope."

From outside I could already hear the high-pitched screaming, relentless, like a soul in torment trapped in a body too small to contain it. I walked out into the hot light of the day and saw his wife, exhausted, her hair soaked from what must've been tears or sweat or both, holding on by threads. Inside the truck was their daughter, just a little girl, but her wide eyes told me she had already seen too much. She was frozen, quiet, scared beyond her years. And then there was the tiny boy, maybe three or four years old. He was screaming like a storm, no one could stop.

When they finally brought him inside, he writhed and screamed, fighting the air, the light, the space, the touch of hands too unsure of what they were doing. The room was chaos. Everyone wanted to fix him, control him, sedate him with love. But none of it was working. The noise was too much. The fear was too loud. So, I asked everyone to leave.

I didn't raise my voice. I didn't shout commands. I just wanted stillness, a moment of peace.

And when I held him, he screamed louder, more wild, more primal than I had ever witnessed in a child so small. My arms became a refuge and a battlefield all at once. I closed my eyes, and I prayed not to silence him but for understanding. And Spirit answered.

A rainbow arched in my inner vision not the sweet, cartoon kind but a pulsing arc of raw color, filled with vibration and frequency. And then the solid, unmistakable knowing arrived without any room for doubt. This child was born into a contract that had nothing to do with quick healing or happy endings. He had an extreme form of autism something sacred, something untouchable by man-made solutions or wishful thinking. His soul, ancient and vast, had agreed to come into this lifetime with a very specific purpose. And I was not written into the contract. My name was not on the paper. My role here was to witness not to rewrite.

Spirit showed me this child was not broken but uniquely built. That what looked like chaos was a language no one in the room had learned how to speak. His soul had chosen this path, not to be healed by another, but to become a mirror. To expose the illusions. To crack open the denial. His screams were not just outbursts; they were vibrations meant to shake the silence of generations. He had power, he had pain, and he had purpose.

But his parents weren't ready. They left hollow, disappointed, angry even. I could feel the ache in their bones, they wanted miracles. Instant softness. They wanted oils and feathers to make the wildness disappear. They expected the sound of singing bowls to soothe their burdened ears. But this wasn't their miracle. Not today.

Spirit showed me something else in the quiet that followed. The opossum doesn't fight fire with fire. It plays dead, not to escape, but to strategize. It survives not with brute force, but by staying invisible, observing, waiting. It adapts. It evolves. And it teaches us to look not just at the obvious path, but at the hidden trails behind the chaos. This family wasn't ready for strategy. They wanted a rescue.

But I was reminded that day that there is sacred power in knowing our role. I was reminded to guard my energy, to honor my place, and to never override the soul agreements of others.

The child was not lost. He was protected. Wild. Ancient. Loud in all the right perfect ways.

conclusion

Many more psychic healing sessions followed too many to list and as my connection to spirit animals deepened, something unexpected began to happen, my connection to myself started to slip. The more I opened to their realm, the more I could feel the fabric of who I thought I was begun to stretch and tear. It was as if I was translating messages for everyone else while forgetting the sound of my own voice. The world I had known, the one that I finally created that made me feel safe, seen, certain, slowly stopped making sense.

The deeper I went into this sacred work, the more lost I felt in my own reflection.

I didn't recognize her. Sometimes I even questioned my God. I didn't know where I belonged.

And so, I asked Spirit. I asked God. I asked my ancestors. Not for more signs, but for something more essential:

Where is home? Where are my people? Where am I in all of this? And in the silence that followed, they came. Not loud. Not in lightning bolts. But in knowing. In fire. In memory.

They came with feathers and wind. With the scent of canela and the smell of herbs and garlic. I could feel the ancient hum of the Aztecs. I could hear the voices of my abuelos and abuelas as if they'd just stepped out of a dream and into my breath.

They reminded me that I had not lost myself. I had simply outgrown the version of me the world had once accepted. I wasn't breaking down. I was breaking open.

The answers I longed for did not come in the form of logic. They came through spirit animals, dreams, visions, in meditations, and in the quiet way truth always arrives when we stop trying to earn it.

And piece by piece, I came home.

To my blood, to my bones, to my lineage, to myself.

I stopped chasing the image the world expected and began honoring the path Spirit carved for me long before I arrived.

I am a curandera.

A medium.

A messenger.

A bridge between worlds.

This book is not just a collection of stories, it is the map of my return.

The animals, the visions, the energy, the healing all of it was part of my remembering.

And maybe, if you found yourself here, they are ready to help you remember too.

Because spirit animals don't visit for no reason.

They arrive when your soul is ready to listen............Just like mine was.

acknowledgements

THANK YOU - To my angels, guides, and ancestors for walking with me, whispering when I couldn't hear, and clapping for me even when this path felt strange and wild. Your presence has been my compass, even in the unknown.

THANK YOU - To all my beautiful clients the souls in this book for trusting me with your stories, your energy, and the messages that came through. You allowed spirit animals to speak, and through you, their wisdom lives on. Thank you for trusting both Ivana and me with your healing journeys. You are the reason this work breathes.

THANK YOU - To Slovakia, my beloved country for embracing my work with open hearts. Your love has turned my five books into bestsellers, and your continued support humbles me every day.

THANK YOU -To our generous sponsors for standing with us as we share this work with the world.

THANK YOU - To my family and my friends all over the world. Thank you for cheering me on when I felt unsure, for grounding me when I felt lost, and for loving me exactly as I am. This book is for all of you.

about the author

Veronica's career path hasn't exactly been traditional but that's what makes it interesting. She started off in Transportation / Freight and logistics, that is how she ended up living in California.

Then she went off to politics, working as a Legislative Assistant for Long Beach Mayor Beverly O'Neill and as a Legislative Analyst for Councilwoman Laura Richardson.

She later became the Community Engagement Director for the American University of Health Sciences, owned and operated two restaurants and bars, and even worked as an event coordinator for a private financial planning firm. In 2015, she graduated from Huntington Academy of Permanent Cosmetics and opened the very first Permanent Cosmetics Studio in Long Beach, California.

Her self-edited and self-published books *My Life My Story, God, You Owe Me* and *Holy Shit* I'm a Fu***ng Psychic* became Amazon's Hot New Releases and bestsellers in the EU, even with all the typos.

She lives with her partner, Ivana Belakova, a world-renowned tattoo artist, Manifestation coach and visionary. Together they travel the world offering positive lifestyle seminars, psychic healing sessions, and transforming outdated mindsets and social barriers.

They also published three children's books: *Meditation for Kids*, *Manifestation for Kids*, and *Visualization for Kids*, which became bestsellers in the EU.

Right now, Veronica splits her time between California and her beloved Slovakia where her ancestors are louder, the spirit animals are clearer, and the healing never stops.